NORTH CAROLINA'S
OCEAN
FISHING
PIERS

From Kitty Hawk to Sunset Beach

AL BAIRD

THE
History
PRESS

Published by The History Press
Charleston, SC 29403
www.historypress.net

Copyright © 2011 by Al Baird
All rights reserved

Cover image by Doug Leister.

First published 2011
Second printing 2012

Manufactured in the United States

ISBN 978.1.60949.148.2

Library of Congress Cataloging-in-Publication Data
Baird, Al.
North Carolina's ocean fishing piers : from Kitty Hawk to Sunset Beach / Al Baird.
p. cm.
Includes bibliographical references.
ISBN 978-1-60949-148-2
1. Saltwater fishing--North Carolina--History. 2. Piers--North Carolina--History. 3. Piers-
-North Carolina--Design and construction--History. 4. North Carolina--History, Local. I.
Title.
SH531.B35 2011
799.1609756--dc22
2011000841

Contents

Foreword

"A labor of love" is one of those phrases that gets thrown around too often. In this case, however, there are no more accurate words to describe this book. In these pages is a seaworthy accumulation of history, anecdotes, photos and fish tales—the most complete story yet assembled about the ocean fishing piers of North Carolina. Prepare to be entertained, informed and amused as Al Baird hooks us on his subject and convinces us that these creosoted castles are indeed worthy of our love.

It's difficult to imagine our beach towns without their piers—but that is the sad reality in Kitty Hawk, Frisco, Indian Beach, Emerald Isle, Long Beach… and who knows where the next one will fall? Like so many endangered species, the public has treated our piers with neglect for far too long. We have taken them for granted, even as we still enjoy their unique role in making the Tar Heel coast such a truly exceptional part of the world.

Al Baird is not like the rest of us. When we saw our favorite piers closing, one after another, and beach access gradually becoming more restricted, we were disappointed. We probably complained. Maybe we got mad.

But Al Baird did far more than just shake his fist. He wrote letters to politicians. He gathered signatures on petitions. He took time away from his own fishing to visit with other anglers and to speak with pier owners about what was happening to their businesses. He organized fishing tournaments to benefit piers. And he founded the North Carolina Fishing Pier Society, which has its own website (ncfps.com) and even a Facebook page.

Al was more than ready to put the labor and the love together. And part of that labor was gathering the stories that make up this book. As he traveled up and down the coast and dug through countless photos in private collections and public archives, he was doing valuable detective work. Every new lead that went into his notebooks sent him off to check out six or ten additional facts. He tirelessly tracked down the old-timers to tell him who built what, who caught what and, most memorably, who said what.

With the publication of *North Carolina's Ocean Fishing Piers*, we now have the most complete history of North Carolina fishing piers ever put between covers. And we owe him our gratitude, because for the past half-century the stories and the history have been disappearing faster than a bag of bloodworms during the spot run.

Sadly, the first generation of pier owners is no longer with us. But fishing piers have always played big roles in small communities, and so there is still a wealth of sources available for someone who takes the time to track them down. Also, piers have often been handed down in families. Thankfully there are still Robertsons, Orrs, Stanleys, Medlins and others who were around when their grandfathers, fathers and uncles built so many of the original sets of planks.

And, thankfully, there are dedicated pier enthusiasts like Al Baird.

I met Al because, twenty years ago, I wrote about a pier marathon that involved myself, my fishing buddy Kim Anderson and photographer Steve Wilson. In a forty-eight-hour period, we fished on every pier between Beaufort Inlet and the South Carolina line. That was twenty-three piers in forty-eight hours, a feat that will never be duplicated because there simply are no longer enough piers. (We scored three before we'd even left Atlantic Beach; only the Oceanana remains.)

Spectator magazine in Raleigh published my story, "Jury of Piers," in August 1990. Over a decade later, when Al and his son set out on a similar mission, he somehow found out about it. He got in touch and later had plaques made so that the North Carolina Fishing Pier Society could recognize our 1990 "World Record Achievement."

Al, being Al, presented the stylish awards to us in person, during a solemn ceremony…held at the Hooters in Morehead City…where we got some great photos…

Ah, but that's a story for another day.

In the pages ahead you'll learn the history of every beachfront pier that's ever been built on the North Carolina coast—how they got started, which hurricanes worked them over and how, in so many cases, they met their ultimate fate. You'll read stories of the most incredible catches, like a 175-pound tarpon and a 1,150-pound tiger shark. Read how not just one, but *two* piers have been plowed into by ships. And learn how one Outer Banks pier was heavily damaged when the wreck of a ship originally sunk in 1889 struck its pilings during a famous nor'easter.

This is a book that needed to be written, illustrated with photos that needed to be collected and preserved. Enjoy this walk down the planks. And promise yourself that one day, just as soon as you can, you will visit one of our twenty or so remaining piers, smell the salt air and maybe add a story of your own to this incomplete tale.

Bill Morris
November 2010
Straits, North Carolina

Bill Morris is the author of the novel *Saltwater Cowboys*. He has written about piers for *Wildlife in North Carolina* magazine, the Raleigh *News and Observer* and *Spectator* magazine.

Acknowledgements

This book could not have been possible without the help of so many people, starting with my fellow members of the North Carolina Fishing Pier Society (NCFPS). They guided and supported me during my many late nights of writing and contributed to my efforts. In particular, thanks to Jack Wood, Brian Cain, Chris Boyles, Dave Finch, Luther Dishman, Bob Langston and Dave Kellough. These hardy fishermen kept checking on the progress of the manuscript and were exceptionally useful in verifying information. Another special thank-you to NCFPS member #1, Bob Goldstein. His books were a valuable reference, and they helped inspire my tours of the piers. His support during the early days of forming the group kept me from giving up.

I would like to thank the pier owners and operators—past and present—who continue to endure bad weather and changing economies. Their fortitude and steadfastness have enabled generations of anglers to have access to the ocean. Those who were especially helpful with this book are Garry Oliver, Greg Ludlum, Doug Medlin, Robin Orr, Matt Johnson and Mike Robertson.

Thanks also to those who helped me research parts of the book. They include Sarah Downing, Kim Cumber, Kelly Fiori, Rose Peters, Madeline Flagler, Christine Jamet, Beverly Tetterton and Wayne Thompson. Special thanks go out to Kari Weinholzer, whom I consulted on the pictures and illustrations for the book, and to my brother, Hugh, whom I was able to get advice from at all hours of the day and night.

ACKNOWLEDGEMENTS

Even more thanks go to Amanda Clark and Ashley Weiderhold, who took the raw pages and formed them into a workable manuscript. My commissioning editor, Jessica Berzon, at The History Press, was always available to answer questions and guide this novice author through the process. I owe her much thanks for her advice and patience.

Thanks to my good friend and fishing buddy Bill Morris; without his tireless assistance, advice, talent and resources I would have never gotten the book completed. He managed to help while simultaneously putting me on more speckled trout and puppy drum than I ever saw in my life. Thanks, Bill.

Finally, thanks to my mother and father, Emma and Al Baird, who instilled a love and appreciation of the North Carolina coast in their four children, and to my wife, Mary, and kids, Katie and Chris, who never seemed to mind spending every vacation at the beach.

This book is dedicated to Mary, my wife, the best catch this fisherman ever made.

Chapter I
The Oldest Pier

KURE PIER (1923)

It was late in the afternoon on Thursday, October 10, 2007, and Mike Robertson, owner of Kure Pier, was looking over the water from the planks of the pier, discussing its rich history. (Kure Pier had just been voted Pier of the Year by the membership of the North Carolina Fishing Pier Society, or NCFPS.) Robertson was talking about his days working out over the water at the end of the pier, making repairs while holding precariously onto a piling. "That is what it was like when you worked for guys like my grandfather and my dad," Robertson beamed.

Kure is recognized as the oldest fishing pier in the state, as well as the oldest still operating on the Atlantic seaboard. But was it the first fishing pier built in the state? Might there have been an earlier pier that did not survive?

Robertson's response is that he does not know, that he once heard there was a pier at Atlantic Beach but he is not sure of any of the details. However, the Carteret County Historical Society asserts that there is no evidence to suggest that there was a pier anywhere on Bogue Banks that would predate the Kure Pier, built in 1923. In fact, it does not show any indication of any piers in the Bogue area until the early 1950s.

This interpretation of factual evidence coincides with the common belief that Mike Robertson's grandfather, L.C. Kure, indeed was the builder of the first ocean fishing pier in North Carolina. And, because it is still in business, today it is certainly the oldest.

But the first pier on the Carolina coast was not at Kure Beach. The Seashore Hotel and Steel Pier were built in 1910 at Wrightsville Beach. Both

The pier at the Seashore Hotel on Wrightsville Beach was the first pier in North Carolina, but it was not used for fishing. The pier was destroyed in a fire in 1920. *Courtesy of the North Carolina State Archives.*

were destroyed by a fire in 1920. However, the Steel Pier wasn't built for fishing; it was for the wealthy people of Wilmington to walk on and take in the sights and the medicinal salt air. At this time, Wilmington was the most cosmopolitan city in North Carolina, Wrightsville Beach being the place where many of the city's elite spent the summer.

Why no one ever thought to fish on the Steel Pier is amusing to Robertson and his guests from the NCFPS. "Probably not something that rich folks did at that time," is one opinion offered.

Robertson's grandfather, L.C. Kure, first built Kure Pier to give beachgoers something to do. The land that the pier is built on has been owned by the family since 1913. In 1915, Kure built a bathhouse on the beach. He then began selling tracts of land and building houses and cottages on the strip of land adjacent to Fort Fisher. The first pier was 120 feet long and 22 feet wide. The fee for fishing was thirty-five cents a day, and a season pass could be purchased for just ten dollars. Untreated pine poles were used as pilings, and sea worms infested them, causing the pier to fall in its first year.

The following year, Kure rebuilt the pier using reinforced concrete. He also extended the length to 240 feet and made it 32 feet wide. Some of these

The Oldest Pier

Kure Pier in the early 1950s, before Hazel destroyed it, had stairs at the end that led down to the water, where smaller boats would ferry people to larger boats anchored offshore. *Courtesy of Mike Robertson.*

pilings were still on the pier when it was purchased by Kure's son-in-law, Bill Robertson, in 1952.

Bill Robertson realized that Kure Pier was under-promoted, so he began to write and photograph events at the pier and around the Kure Beach area. His articles and stories ran in newspapers across the state. They made the North Carolina coast inviting to people on farms or from small towns farther inland. With increasing wages and improvements made in the roads, a visit to Kure Beach was a real possibility in the 1950s.

At the same time, Aycock Brown, the director of the Dare County Tourist Bureau, was promoting beaches in the northern part of the state. Working independently of one another, Robertson and Brown portrayed the beauty and excitement of the coastal waters in North Carolina to the eastern half of the nation at a time when working families were increasing their level of disposable income.

The first major land boom for beach property in North Carolina occurred in the 1950s. Coastal communities sprung up on every barrier island, and the number of fishing piers multiplied from six in 1950 to thirty by the time the decade ended. What made this boom even more impressive was that during this time, North Carolina had rightly earned the nickname "Hurricane Alley." Several major storms, including Hurricanes Hazel (1954), Connie and Diane (both 1955), made landfall and pummeled the shore. The storms tore down piers almost as fast as they could be built.

The Kure Pier was no exception. In 1953, Robertson spent $15,000 to revamp the pier, extending it to over 900 feet. As luck would have it, Hazel then destroyed the pier the following year. Once again, Robertson rebuilt it. Instead of duplicating the destroyed pier, Robertson made changes to the pier house, including the addition of a bingo room and an open-air dance hall, and extended the pier to 880 feet. The rebuilt pier, which Robertson continued to promote, was reopened in 1955.

Kure Pier after it was rebuilt after Hazel. Bill Robertson took the photo from the water tower at Kure Beach and noted after, "That is when I discovered I had a fear of heights." *Courtesy of Mike Robertson.*

The Oldest Pier

Kure Pier was producing fish and making headlines throughout the state. Fishermen Clyde Leonard, A. D. Roach, Roy Fulk and Homer Holman of Lexington, North Carolina, hauled in 150 pounds of spots and whiting, according to an article in the October 29, 1957 edition of the *Dispatch*, a Lexington newspaper that often featured articles written by Bill Robertson.

A year before Hurricane Hazel, Harvey Williams took two hours to deck a fifty-pound tarpon. Several other tarpon were reportedly caught at the pier around the same time. Tarpon were probably the most sought-after big game fish, but king mackerel fishing would soon become even more popular.

Fishing continued to be good for the next two decades. On an early July day in 1972, David Arthur of Wilmington, North Carolina, caught four kings ranging in weight from twelve to fifteen pounds. Arthur's catch began a week during which over twenty-five kings were caught.

Over the years, Kure Pier has continued to deck its share of big fish. In 1978, Stanley Seawell, twenty-four, from Robbins, North Carolina, caught a state record 421-pound, eight-ounce lemon shark. This record still holds today, and Seawell worked hard for it, battling the fish for two hours before landing it. He carved up the shark and gave the meat away, providing shark dinners for dozens of people. According to the July 8, 1978 article in the *Wilmington Morning Star*, angler Seawell was inspired by the movie *Jaws*, but he did not claim to "need a bigger pier."

Kure Pier was home to one of the most enduring records for saltwater fish. On October 10, 1931, Mrs. A. L. Freeman caught a three-pound, four-ounce sea mullet. She held the state record all by herself until it was tied in 1970 and then broken in 1971 by a three-pound, eight-ounce sea mullet caught at the Iron Steamer Pier.

In 1984, after Hurricane Diana tore down half of Kure Pier, Mike Robertson bought the pier from his father Bill. The fishing on Kure Pier was good, even while the structure was being rebuilt. While repairing the pier the following spring, one of the workmen, Jack Hoops of Bluefield, Virginia, caught a seventeen-pound, nine-ounce bluefish.

After Diana, Mike Robertson rebuilt the pier to 711 feet and added a "T" at the end to enhance king fishing. Nearly ninety years after it was first built, it remains a favorite among anglers and has a loyal following. Bob Holbrook, from Charlotte, is a typical fan. Born in 1948, he has been fishing the pier since he was twelve. "I raised two sons at the pier, and they love it also," Holbrook boasts.

There is no denying the popularity of the pier. Local resident Lisa Tsangarides considers the pier to be the "focal point of Kure Beach." She cites the generosity of Mike and Lisa Robertson in "making it available to all kinds of charity fishing tournaments." Dawson Freuler agrees and adds, "Mike does an incredible job making sure the pier is a great place for families to fish."

Today, Kure Pier remains one of the most affordable and enjoyable places to fish on the entire coast. The pier house has a gift shop, a bait and tackle shop and a snack bar with an ice cream stand. The pier is the official sponsor of both the Youth Pier Fishing Tournament and the Disabled Fisherman Tournament.

Chapter 2
The Early Years
1936–1949

FORT FISHER FISHING PIER (1936–1954)

In the late 1930s, brothers Louis B. and Thomas R. Orrell purchased most of the land at the south end of Pleasure Island, which lies between Snow's Cut on the north and the Cape Fear River and includes Carolina Beach and Kure Beach.

In 1936, Walter Winner constructed a one-thousand-foot fishing pier there. Ironically, this pier was only a short distance from the only other pier in the state, Kure Pier. Fort Fisher Fishing Pier featured a tackle store and a restaurant. The daily fishing rate in 1946 was thirty-five cents.

The pier was destroyed by Hurricane Hazel and never rebuilt. But even a broken fishing pier provides structure to attract fish, and as late as the mid-1970s the wreck of the Fort Fisher Fishing Pier was known as a popular spot for speckled sea trout. Some anglers would float boats out to fish over the pier's remains. Fort Fisher Fishing Pier lives on today only in postcards.

JOHNNIE MERCER'S PIER (1937–   )

In 1937, Julian Morton built North Carolina's third ocean pier, the Atlantic View Fishing Pier in Wrightsville Beach. Luther Rogers bought the pier from Morton and then sold it to Johnnie Mercer in 1939. Mercer had wanted to build his own pier earlier but was turned down by the town. After taking over the Atlantic View, he changed the name of the pier to Johnnie Mercer's Pier in the early 1940s.

An illustrated postcard depicting the Fort Fisher Pier in the 1930s. The pier was destroyed by Hazel and was not rebuilt. *Courtesy of New Hanover Public Library, Robert M. Fales Collection.*

One popular urban legend is that Mercer was the famous singer/songwriter Johnny Mercer who penned several hit songs, including "Moon River." This myth is widely believed, but it is not true. Their first names are spelled differently, and the famous Johnny Mercer was likely never even on the pier.

Johnnie Mercer, the pier owner, worked the pier night and day until he was killed in an automobile accident in 1964. His widow, Wanda Nuckols Mercer, ran the pier until 1969 and then sold it to Bob Johnson. Johnson's son Matt now owns and operates the pier.

Bob Langston, from Asheboro, North Carolina, grew up on the Virginia peninsula. As a child, he would vacation with his family at Wrightsville Beach. Langston recalls that from 1963 until 1970 his family would rent an apartment for one week one block north of Mercer's pier. Langston's grandmother, who lived in Wilmington, would catch a green and yellow bus that would take her to Wrightsville, so she could visit with the family while they vacationed.

Langston recalls what Mercer's was like at that time: "Our walks on the pier were adventures for me. The pier house was a magic place for a four-year-old. There were Skee-Ball machines that even I could play. There were other arcade games and a jukebox. On the left was that magic lunch counter

A postcard of the entrance ramp at Johnnie Mercer's Pier from the early 1960s. *Courtesy of Matt Johnson.*

Prior to buses bringing beachgoers to Wrightsville Beach from Wilmington, the trolley would do the job. *Courtesy of the Wrightsville Beach Museum.*

with great burgers, hot dogs and crinkle-cut French fries. Overhead hung the rigs of the regulars...long rods with big reels. I always felt like it was the coolest place on earth."

Like many North Carolina piers, Mercer's Pier has had its share of damage from storms. Hurricane Hazel virtually destroyed it in 1954, and then a year later Hurricane Connie wiped it out again. The 1996 hurricane duo of Bertha and Fran, which dealt so much damage, closed Mercer's Pier. But unlike so many others, Mercer's was rebuilt—although not without a battle with the town fathers of Wrightsville. In 2002, Johnnie Mercer's Pier finally reopened after a lengthy legal fight over a permit issue that pertained to the size of the new pier house.

The new pier that opened in 2002 is like no other in the state. It is 760 feet long and made of steel-reinforced concrete. The loss of most piers to storms is due to the tidal surge coming up from below and lifting the decking structure off the pilings. Not only will Mercer's Pier be hard to lift because of the concrete, but the center of the pier has steel grates that the powerful waves can come up through, reducing the stress on the rest of the pier. The sides of the pier gently slope down and are also made of concrete. At the bottom there are vents that allow any water that does come up to the deck to drain out the sides.

The first thing you notice when you walk out onto a concrete pier is that the pier doesn't move. Wooden piers are designed to move with the waves; this helps them survive rough seas. Mercer's Pier doesn't budge.

There are also subtle differences between traditional wooden piers and concrete piers that affect the fishing itself. On a concrete pier, you cannot carve out a notch for your pole to rest in. Most experienced anglers bring a towel or rag to lean the pole against. Additionally, the concrete pilings make it harder for anglers to snag their hooks on them, so less terminal tackle is lost.

Veteran angler James Neal, of Wrightsville Beach, cites other differences. "Certain types of fish are attracted to the concrete," Neal says. "Barracudas, for one. Also, the pilings are thirty feet apart and on wooden piers they are twelve, so there aren't as many sheepshead here as there would be at other piers." (Sheepshead congregate around pier pilings, where they pick at barnacles and small bait fish.)

Johnnie Mercer's Pier has even been the site of marine research. In the mid-1980s, biologists conducted a controlled study, placing fifteen five-foot-tall, six-foot-wide plastic devices in the water at the end of both Mercer's Pier and the Crystal Pier. The idea was to see if these devices would attract and improve the number of big fish caught. This study, however, was

Mercer's caught its share of big fish. Here is Frank Larkin with a large king mackerel. *Courtesy of Matt Johnson.*

inconclusive. Indeed, the artificial reefs increased the number of baitfish in the area, and flounder catches were up, but there was no evidence that they improved the king mackerel fishing.

In the early 1970s, Mercer's reputation was as good as any for big game fish. Often the pier would deck over twenty kings in a single day. In October 1971, a forty-eight-pound king was weighed in. The pier has also laid claim to some nice amberjacks, cobia and bluefish. In July 1980, Ray Riggs landed six kings in one day. In 1984, both a fifty-pound and an eighty-one-pound amberjack were planked, and in 1993, an angler decked a forty-four-pound black-tip shark.

The Wrightsville Beach area is popular with surfers as it provides some of the biggest waves in the southeast part of the state. However, with big waves come rip currents, from which several people have had to be rescued over the years. In 1973, a three-year-old boy fell off the pier and into the strong current. Three fishermen dove off the pier and into the ocean. They pulled the boy to a piling and waited to be pulled out of the water.

While most piers close for the winter months and reopen sometime after March 1, Mercer's Pier is one of the few to stay open year round, allowing anglers to indulge their passion. Drum (both red and black) and speckled trout can be found during the winter. Tony Costagliola, from Wilmington, North Carolina, has been fishing the Wrightsville Beach area and Mercer's Pier for sixteen years. He says that just because the temperature drops the fishing doesn't stop. "Last December my son-in-law and I caught 105 puffers here in a day," Costagliola said. "So, you just never know."

For the last five years, Mercer's Pier has kicked off the season by holding the JMP's Dogfish tournament in late January. The tournament was started by two of the regulars, Rick Britt and Arlen Ash. Britt holds two pier records for red drum (32 pounds) and sea mullet (2.57 pounds). Ash holds the record for tarpon with a 158-pound fish, caught in September 2005.

So, why would two accomplished big game fishermen start a tournament targeting dogfish? "We were looking for one day out of the winter to get together and see our fishing buddies," Britt said.

The idea of hosting a winter tournament soon caught on. Today, the event is attended by pier anglers from all over the East Coast who are looking for an excuse to get out over the water during the winter months. The 2009 JMP's Dogfish tournament champion, Matt McKinney, said, "I came out with no expectations. I never thought I would have so much fun. The group of people there were great."

Mercer's Pier is open twenty-four hours a day, 365 days a year. The pier sells tackle and bait and has a full-service grill, an arcade and a gift shop.

CRYSTAL PIER (1939–1996)

Two years after the construction of the Atlantic View Fishing Pier (soon to be Johnnie Mercer's), and only 1.7 miles down the beach, the Mira Mar Pier was erected by Floyd Cox. The pilings of the Mira Mar Pier were made of cypress, and the pier was built over the wreck of a Confederate blockade runner, the *Fanny and Genny*.

The Mira Mar Pier has endured several name changes over the years. It was first renamed the Luna Pier, in hopes that its name would draw attention to the nearby tourist attraction and dance hall Lumina. Luna Pier then became Crystal Pier in 1940, when restaurant owner Mike Zezefellis bought it from the Hutaff family. Zezefellis was a Greek immigrant who owned the pier for thirty years. In the 1970s, Zezefellis sold Crystal Pier to his cousins, Nick and George Fokakis. In 1989, the pier was sold to Monica Wells, who added the Oceanic Restaurant and changed the name of the pier to the Oceanic Pier.

Beachgoers and surf fishermen on Wrightsville Beach at the Mira Mar Pier in Wrightsville Beach. The pier had several names over the years, and often anglers used the names interchangeably. *Courtesy of the Wrightsville Beach Museum.*

During World War II, the pier house was used as an army patrol station for soldiers guarding the coast. Residents of Wrightsville Beach would later recall that if you went to the beach at night, you were likely to end up on the wrong end of a soldier's gun.

Local fishermen long believed that the Crystal Pier's location just north of Masonboro Inlet was one of the reasons it was so productive. Another reason they felt it was superior to other piers was the remains of the *Fanny and Genny* wreck that had, over time, become an artificial reef. Whatever the reason, Crystal Pier has produced many nice catches over the years.

Rodney Barnes, from Greensboro, was fifteen when he first went to Wrightsville. He stayed with his uncle and aunt while his parents went to Myrtle Beach. Barnes met a lot of locals through his cousin, and he stayed with his new friends during the summers and breaks from school. One of his best friends was and still is Bubba Cox, whose grandfather, Floyd Cox, built the original Mira Mar Pier. Bubba Cox and his family still had a house next door to the pier.

"They had a guest room upstairs with basically my name on it, as I spent as much time there during summers as I did in Greensboro," Barnes recalled.

"The target fish then as today were Spanish and kings, which were quite plentiful. Actually, the first king tournament at Wrightsville Beach was won by Bubba Cox, who caught the largest king from Crystal back in the summer of either 1969 or 1970." Barnes agrees with the conventional wisdom that Crystal Pier's close location to the inlet is one reason the pier has been so productive. These days, Rodney Barnes takes his son to Wrightsville and still fishes with his old friend Bubba Cox. But they do their fishing from Mercer's Pier.

After damage inflicted by Hurricane Felix in 1995 and then by Bertha and Fran in 1996, only a short piece of the Crystal Pier remains. Once one thousand feet in length, Crystal Pier is now closed; however, the Oceanic Restaurant is still open, and the remaining part of the pier has been converted for outdoor dining and receptions.

Michael Johnson, now of Myrtle Beach, has several memories of the pier, including the time he saw a 20/0 reel (which would be about ten inches in diameter). "Squeeky Kelly had one, when he tried to hook up Ol' George," Johnson said. Ol' George was an eighteen-foot hammerhead shark with a head that was five feet wide. The giant used to cruise Wrightsville Beach—unseen, one assumes, by the thousands of swimmers on the beach.

These days Matt Brooks, from Wilmington, fishes the Oak Island Pier, but he said he first set foot on Crystal Pier in 1992. Brooks, who at that time was living in Connecticut, was down for a week's vacation. He had spotted three large fish in the water and remembers thinking they were sharks. The man fishing next to him told him they were cobia. Brooks tossed his gotcha plug at them, and the smallest one hit it. He ended up catching a thirty-six-inch cobia. When Brooks returned home, he put in his two weeks' notice at his job and moved to Wilmington. "My boss asked me where I was going to work," Brooks remembered. "I told him I had four job offers and was going to take the one that paid the best."

The popularity of fishing piers often goes hand in hand with the number of big fish caught on the pier. Crystal Pier has had its share of monstrous fish, including some record breakers. The year 1961 was a memorable one for Bobby Kentrolis and the Crystal Pier; Kentrolis caught a then state record 152-pound tarpon, as well as a 478-pound blue shark. The blue shark is still a record today.

In July 1973, retired U.S. Army lieutenant colonel J.W. Feilder, of Wilmington, North Carolina, hooked a sixty-two-pound tarpon on spinning tackle spooled with a fifteen-pound test. A sixty-two-pound cobia was caught in 1979 by Tom Snyder from Raleigh, North Carolina. Pier regular Charlie Herring, of Wilmington, North Carolina, caught a sixty-three-pound,

The Crystal Pier suffered damage from many storms over the years, starting with Hurricane Hazel in 1954. *Courtesy of the North Carolina State Archives.*

eleven-ounce tarpon in July 1983. Chris Hager, also of Wilmington, decked a forty-one-pound king in July 1987.

Crystal Pier not only had to contend with storms, but it also had to contend with damage from a boat. In August 1980, a forty-eight-foot fishing boat called the *Explorer* hit Crystal Pier just after midnight, leaving a forty-by twenty-foot hole in the pier. James Neal was one of the people on the planks when the *Explorer* hit.

"He [the captain] had it on autopilot and fell asleep," Neal recalled, "Some of us were out on the end of the pier, and the ship hit the pier about three-quarters of the way out. We had to carry our equipment across the only stringer (a beam that runs parallel to the pier) that was left." Fortunately, there were no injuries.

Despite his misadventure that night, James Neal still has a fondness in his heart for the old Crystal Pier. Standing on Mercer's Pier looking south toward the Oceanic Restaurant, he stares into the past and says, "If I ever become rich, I am going to buy that pier and build it back out. That was one fine fishing pier."

JENNETTE'S PIER (1939–2003, 2011?–   )

People have been vacationing in Nags Head on the Outer Banks of North Carolina since the 1750s, when rich farmers and plantation owners from eastern North Carolina and southern Virginia would send their families there. They did this not only for the rest and relaxation of the shore in the summertime but also to protect them from malaria and to be healed by the magical salt waters of the Atlantic Ocean. By the 1850s, the primitive cottages of Nags Head were joined by real luxury accommodations. You could spend a whole month at the Nags Head Hotel for twenty dollars, including meals.

The Nags Head Hotel had a pier that extended out into the Pamlico Sound, but like the Steel Pier in Wrightsville, this pier was not for fishing. Instead, it was used to haul people and their belongings over the shallow waters of the sound. The hotel featured a horse-drawn railroad, which would ferry people over to the ocean so they could spend the day in the sun and dip themselves in the healing waters of the Atlantic. During the Civil War, the Nags Head Hotel was used by the Confederate army as headquarters. When they were forced to retreat, the Confederates destroyed the hotel to keep the Union army from using it.

It wasn't until the later part of the nineteenth century that the Outer Banks became widely known for outstanding fishing. Most of that fishing was done from boats using nets, but Edward R. Outlaw Jr. reported in his 1956 book, *Old Nags Head*, that "bluefish of large size were caught with squid and hook in the surf."

In 1939, Walton Jennette, a businessman from Elizabeth City, North Carolina, built Jennette's Ocean Pier. The pier cost $6,000 and was the first pier in North Carolina to be built north of Wilmington and the first of five that would be built on an eighteen-mile stretch of the northern Outer Banks. The rooms and apartments that flanked the pier were built during the Great Depression to house Civilian Conservation Corps workers who were building the barrier dunes from the Virginia state line to Ocracoke. After the pier was built, the rooms were rented to vacationers. The Depression-era buildings were finally razed in the 1990s.

The first Jennette's Pier would last three years before sea worms had their way with the structure. By that time, America was in the middle of World War II, and the pier would have to wait to be rebuilt. Finally, in 1947, Jennette's Pier was reconstructed.

In the 1960s and 1970s, Jennette's Pier became the home of some of the East Coast's most serious shark fishermen. Using their heavy reels and lines,

Jennette's Pier in 1950. The pier at that time featured a second T at just over the halfway point. The land south of the pier was still vacant. *Courtesy of the Outer Banks History Center, Roger Meekins, photographer.*

they often would bag a trophy blue shark, dusky or hammerhead. Shark clubs in North Carolina and Virginia made Jennette's Pier their home base, as it was one of the few piers that allowed shark fishing.

Danny Daniels, from St. Albans, West Virginia, remembers being on the pier when the Virginia Beach Sharkers showed up. "Those guys were crazy," Daniels recalls. "They would do anything to catch a big shark. They hung tuna carcasses from both corners of the pier. Then they lowered someone in a makeshift raft and had him paddle bait out guiding him with a flashlight."

Daniels recalls that one of the guys caught a three-hundred-pound lemon shark. Daniels watched the sharker work on his catch for over two hours, cutting it up and removing its jaw. "I will remember it for the rest of my life," Daniels says.

In 1960, Robert T. Keller caught a 710-pound hammerhead shark and then followed it up in 1963 by bagging a 610-pound dusky shark. Both catches still hold the state records in North Carolina. The Department of Marine Fisheries has the Nags Head Pier recorded as the location of Keller's catches; in his book *Pier Fishing in North Carolina*, author Bob Goldstein reports it as

Jennette's Pier. "It was frustrating," said Sarah Downing, assistant curator of the Outer Banks History Center, who had previously researched the location of Keller's catches for her publications. "This book [by Goldstein] says one thing and the DMF website says another."

This discrepancy can be solved by a visit to the Outer Banks History Center. The center has the proof to confirm that Bob Goldstein's account of Keller's record-breaking catches is correct. David Stick, who, along with his father, Frank Stick, had more to do with the establishment of the Cape Hatteras National Seashore National Park than anyone else, donated his files to the center. Stick was a local writer and historian, and the files that he donated to the center contain pictures by Aycock Brown showing Keller with the record-breaking sharks. The sharks are tagged with their weight, and a "Jennette's Pier" sign is clearly visible in each picture.

During his long career with the Dare County Tourism Bureau, Aycock Brown's photography drew more and more people to the Outer Banks.

Robert Keller from Cleveland, Ohio, stands next to his 710-pound hammerhead shark caught at Jennette's that is still a record today. *Courtesy of the Outer Banks History Center, Aycock Brown, photographer.*

The Early Years

North Carolina native Matthew Bateman's grandparents often took him and his two brothers to Nags Head, where they would fish from Jennette's Pier. "They thought it was important to take us to the pier," Bateman remembered. "I pretty much grew up on Jennette's, and I have always had a love for pier fishing."

Jennette's Pier has had its share of damage over the years. In 1962, the notorious nor'easter called the Ash Wednesday Storm completely destroyed the pier. Earlier, in 1960, Hurricane Donna smashed a ship's hull right through the center of it. But that would not be Jennette's last, or weirdest, encounter with a shipwreck. The Graveyard of the Atlantic had another trick up its sleeve.

On October 23, 1889, the vessel *Francis E. Waters* went to the bottom of the ocean off Nags Head. The 147-ton schooner and its crew and cargo of lumber were lost. It remained in place for almost ninety years, until the wreck washed ashore just north of Jennette's Pier in January 1978. In late April of the same year, another storm washed the *Francis E. Waters* back out to sea—and the ghost ship then began to float slowly toward the pier. On the afternoon of April 27, 1978, the keel of the ship slammed into the middle section of Jennette's Pier and worked its way through the structure, knocking out a fifty-four-foot section of the pier. The *Francis E. Waters* continued to float south, barely missing the Outer Banks Pier, before coming to rest at the Oregon Inlet Campground. The remains of the *Francis E. Waters* are now on display at the Nags Head Municipal Building.

Jennette's Pier was repaired and reopened after its shipwreck encounter, but it would continue to do battle with storms into the new century. Hurricane Emily destroyed the pier in 1993. In 1996, $400,000 worth of renovations were completed. However, the series of storms in the late 1990s did extensive damage, and by 2002, Jennette's Pier was in need of a buyer who could keep it open. Prospects of linking it to a hotel were offered, but the details could not be worked out. Finally, in late 2002, the pier was rescued by the North Carolina Aquarium Society, a nonprofit organization that received grant money to buy and fix the pier.

Jennette's Pier was nearly six hundred feet long when it reopened in 2003. The refurbished pier featured displays and exhibits from the North Carolina Aquarium in Manteo. But just as the pier was regaining popularity, Hurricane Isabel made landfall as a Category 2 storm near Drum Inlet on the Core Banks. Isabel's 105-mile-per-hour winds built a storm surge that cut a new inlet between the villages of Frisco and Hatteras and damaged houses, businesses and fishing piers all along the Outer Banks.

Hurricane Isabel sheared off 550 feet of Jennette's Pier and severely damaged the pier house, and the pier once again closed. The North Carolina Aquarium Society drew up plans to replace the pier with a concrete structure. The design was based on Johnnie Mercer's Pier in Wrightsville Beach. The North Carolina Aquarium Society then set out to find $18 million to fund the project.

By 2007, efforts to obtain the funding needed to rebuild Jennette's Pier had stalled, and the pier's future seemed in doubt. Fortunately, North Carolina had set up the Waterfront Access Study Committee (WASC), which was responsible for looking into issues affecting public access and working waterfronts. Fishing piers fell under the jurisdiction of the WASC, and Jennette's Pier received $1.5 million to start construction.

In order to receive this funding, Jennette's Pier would have to be a state-owned entity. So in 2007 it was transferred from the North Carolina Aquarium Society to the North Carolina Aquariums, part of the North Carolina Department of Cultural Resources. The new plans call for a pier one thousand feet in length, made of wood set on steel-reinforced concrete pilings able to withstand hurricane winds of up to 130 miles per hour. The pier house will be sixteen thousand square feet and powered by wind and solar power. The new pier and pier house will cost over $25 million, and their construction was one of the first bills new Governor Beverly Purdue signed into law.

A controversy arose over the naming of the pier, although it has been referred to as the Jennette's Pier Project all along. When the bill passed through the state legislature, the name on the pier was the "North Carolina Aquarium Pier at Nags Head." The disapproval was almost instant. Over one thousand people signed an online petition, and the Town of Nags Head passed a resolution encouraging the North Carolina Aquariums to incorporate "Jennette's Pier" into the name.

The public won the debate, and the pier will be called the North Carolina Aquarium's Jennette's Pier. Regardless of the name, anglers like Matthew Bateman are thrilled. "I can't wait," he said.

Construction started in the summer of 2009 and has continued to progress. The planned opening date is May 2011. Two more state-run piers are planned—one at Emerald Isle and the other at Carolina Beach. Each pier is near one of the state's aquarium locations and will be made of reinforced concrete, not wood.

Nags Head Fishing Pier (1947–)

While visitors to Nags Head had to wait almost two hundred years for its first ocean fishing pier—Jennette's—a second opened up only eight years later. When Jennette's Pier was going through its first rebuild, the Mann's Ocean Pier was being erected just over six miles to the north. The pier was built by Gaston Mann, who was strong and stout and notched the pilings himself. He would later name his creation Nags Head Pier.

As with so many piers, Mann's had attractions that went well beyond fishing. A roller-skating rink attached to the pier house—and called "Ocean Shores Recreation Center"—was built right after the pier was constructed. Mann owned the pier and the recreation center until his death in the mid-1960s.

Dave and Rita Mizelle owned the Nags Head Fishing Pier at the time of the famous Ash Wednesday Storm. The epic nor'easter left only about fifteen pilings left at the center of where the pier had stood. The Mizelles recovered as many of the pilings as possible and then took out a Small Business Administration loan and rebuilt. Rita Mizelle told a reporter from

Nags Head Pier in 1950 featured Mann's Recreation Center to the right of the pier. It was a popular attraction and offered roller skating and arcade games. *Courtesy of the Outer Banks History Center, Roger Meekins, photographer.*

Rita Mizelle, who owned the pier along with her husband in the 1960s, was quite the sportsman herself. Here she is holding a 24.5-pound bluefish that was caught in 1971. It established a women's world record. *Courtesy of the Outer Banks History Center, Aycock Brown, photographer.*

the *OBX Sentinel*, "We paid it [the loan] off before the due date and put the pier back immediately."

In the 1970s, the Nags Head Fishing Pier was owned by Joe Justius, who had sold a machine shop in his native Pennsylvania to purchase the pier. Since the late 1950s, the Nags Head Fishing Pier has advertised "Fishing Day and Night" and rented cottages and utility apartments.

In 1976, Terry Mosley, now a teacher of North Carolina history at North Carolina Central University in Durham, took a summer off from college to work for Justius. "I worked as a counter hand, fixed rental fishing gear, bagged bait, waited on customers and anything else I was asked, including hosing down the bathroom. Joe had the bathrooms tiled from top to bottom with a floor drain installed and had me blast them clean every morning with a power washer so he could brag about having the cleanest bathrooms of any fishing pier," Mosley said.

Mosley also remembered that Justius had someone clean the beach on either side of the pier each day. "While Daddy is fishing, Momma is laying on the beach and if it is clean they'll be back," Justius would preach. When the fishing got slow, Justius would send his counter help out with lures called jerk jiggers, which they made at the pier for very little cost, and have them try to snag some blues. Mosley or the others would make a very big deal of it if they snagged one, which encouraged the bottom fishers who weren't having any luck to run into the pier to buy the lures.

That year (1976), on July 31, Justius held a fishing tournament at the pier for fifty kids from Governor Morehead School for the Blind. The tournament was called the Project Sight Fishing Tournament, and it raised money for treatments, Braille typewriters and other resources and services needed by the blind.

A favorite hangout of the pier hands and charter boat crews was Sam and Omie's, a restaurant right across from Jennette's Pier. The restaurant was owned by Tom and John McKimmey, who purchased it from Sam Tillet. Tillet was a commercial fisherman who, in the late 1930s, started offering charter fishing cruises to sportsmen. After the war, Tillet decided to sell charters out of his restaurant. Tillet eventually decided to do the charters full time and sold the restaurant to the McKimmeys.

The restaurant gave discounts to locals or summer help. Mosley remembers, "It had a couple of pool tables and cheap draft beer." Mosley also remembers that "the food was excellent, and you didn't have to contend with too many tourists after being around them all day." Sam and Omie's is still in business and is still a favorite of Nags Head locals and visitors alike.

Today, at 740 feet, Nags Head Fishing Pier is the longest on the Outer Banks. A sign at the entrance of the pier says, "The Happiest People in the World Pass thru This Door." Judging by the amount of smiles one encounters on the pier, the sign might be right. One of the reasons people are so happy is because Nags Head Fishing Pier is a fun and productive fishing spot.

Kings in the forty-pound range are common. In 1982, fifteen kings were landed. Witnesses say they think over forty had been hooked. So many large bluefish have been caught at Nags Head Fishing Pier that a great bluefish catch is considered routine. The pier gets more than its fair share of cobia, and around winter, when the water cools, striped bass have been known to make an appearance.

In 1993, a 65-pound amberjack was decked. That same year, an $8^3/_4$-pound Spanish proved to be the largest of the North Carolina fishing season. In late June 1994, a 72-pound cobia and a 58-pound king mackerel were reportedly

In the 1970s and 1980s, the piers on the Outer Banks were as good as you could get for king mackerel. *Courtesy of the Outer Banks History Center, Ray Couch, photographer.*

caught off the pier. In 1996, another 72-pounder was decked. In 1997, Stuart Hale of Gates City, Virginia, caught a 75-pound cobia.

Andy McCann took over ownership of the pier and restaurant in 1987 and is the current owner. He enclosed the deck on the back of the pier house and redecorated it. The pier has a full-service restaurant, which will clean and cook your catch. The pier sells tackle and bait and has rental fishing rods and reels. There are also apartments and cottages that can be rented by the day or week.

CAROLINA BEACH FISHING PIER (1947–   )

Located on Pleasure Island, just south of Wilmington, Carolina Beach Fishing Pier was built at the far north end of Carolina Beach. Because of its location, the pier is commonly called North Pier. It is located right next to Freeman's Park. Before World War I, and before the sound was dredged, the location of the pier was occupied by an inlet.

Above: Carolina Beach Pier is also known as the North End Pier due to its position at the edge of the town of Carolina Beach. Freeman Park is located to the north of the pier and is popular with surf fishermen. *Courtesy of New Hanover Public Library,* Star-News *Archives.*

Right: Fishermen crowd the planks on the Carolina Beach Pier in 1950. It was the first of three piers built in Carolina Beach. *Courtesy of the North Carolina State Archives.*

The Carolina Beach Fishing Pier is built over a rocky bottom near Snow's Cut and Carolina Beach Inlet. This location gives the pier an advantage, as it attracts certain types of fish, like flounder and sheepshead. The pier is perhaps the tallest (above sea level) on the coast and is currently owned by the Phelps family.

The Carolina Beach Fishing Pier was owned by Sam Blake in the mid-1960s and was considered back then to be out in the boondocks. Blake's successor, Thomas J. Jackson Jr., promoted his pier by claiming that it spanned the "Longest, Widest and Deepest Water in North Carolina." Jackson also built a campground, but by the mid-1980s, it was gone, and motels had sprung up in its place.

Betty Jo Phelps moved to Carolina Beach in the late 1970s with her husband, Fred, who decided to buy the pier after Betty Jo had gone fishing on it. Later, they would build the nearby North End Condos and help develop the northern part of the island. Fred died in 1995, and when the Carolina Beach Fishing Pier was destroyed by Bertha and Fran in 1996, Phelps's son, Freddie, rebuilt it as it stands today.

The Carolina Beach Fishing Pier has caught its share of large fish. Black drum, cobia and an array of kings have all been claimed by the pier's anglers. In July 1973, a forty-five-pound king mackerel was decked. In October 1980, twenty-eight kings were pulled from the ocean. In June 1985, David Robinson, an employee of the pier, took some time off work and landed three king mackerel in a single day. In 1987, Dave Mercer and Johnny Bullard, both of Wilmington, landed a pair of amberjacks that were sixty-six and sixty-four pounds.

Si Cantwell now regularly fishes the Carolina Beach Fishing Pier with his wife, whom he describes as the "master fisherman" of the Cantwell family. Cantwell started fishing from North Carolina piers when he was seven years old. He first visited a pier on a family vacation, when his grandfather took him to a pier near Salter Path. Cantwell recalls his first cast: "I remember pulling my rod and Zebco reel back and casting out as far as I could. Unfortunately, I crossed the lines of a good two dozen fishermen. Granddaddy and I worked the pole over the heads of the fishermen, walking out to the one fisherman whose line was utterly tangled with mine. The man patiently helped my grandfather pull our lines apart, then taught me the underhanded casting method that was much more appropriate for a boy my age."

The Carolina Beach Fishing Pier has a tackle store that rents rods and reels. It also features a great second-story view from the grill. In addition to being a great fishing spot, the pier is a popular location for weddings and other celebrations.

Chapter 3
The Golden Era of Pier Construction

1950–1960

SURF CITY PIER (1951–   )

The North Carolina coast has a rich history, and Topsail Island's (pronounced Topsil) history is perhaps richer than any other barrier island in the state. In the early 1700s, it was supposed to have been the playground of Edward Teach, aka Blackbeard the Pirate, and others of his ilk. During the Civil War, Topsail Island was part of the Union blockade of the South, and several blockade runners were sunk off its shores. In the 1930s, the island was the location of a celebrated treasure hunt by a group of investors from New York who were trying to find gold from a Spanish galleon sunk in 1750.

During the Second World War, the U.S. Army set up Camp Davis on Topsail and used it as a training location for antiaircraft target practice. The army used members of its Women's Airforce Service Pilot Corp, or WASPs, to pull target gliders behind their planes, and then the infantrymen on the ground would fire at the gliders.

After the war, the U.S. Navy took over Camp Davis and used it for developing its surface-to-air guided missile program, code named Project Bumblebee. Observation towers were built along the beach to track the flight of the ramjet rockets. Many of these square concrete towers are still standing. By 1948, they were outgunning their range, so the navy sought another location, and the operation on Topsail was closed down. Rocket development moved to Cape Canaveral, Florida.

A pontoon bridge had been established in Surf City to aid the army's and navy's efforts to move material and personnel. This bridge was left intact and helped accelerate the development of the island after the military moved. Surf City was incorporated in 1949.

Surf City Ocean Pier was built in 1951, and it was the first of nine piers eventually to be built on the twenty-six miles of Topsail coastline between New River Inlet and New Topsail Inlet. The Surf City Pier, built by H.B. Barwick, was originally a steel pier, and in ads for the pier in the 1950s and 1960s, it claimed (incorrectly) the honors of being North Carolina's first and longest steel pier. After being wrecked by a nor'easter in 1973, the pier was converted to wood.

For the last thirty-six years, the pier has been owned by two generations of the Lore family, who bought it in 1973.

Most of the major storms took their toll on the Surf City Pier. The pier was destroyed by Hazel; Gloria, Bertha and Fran also did significant damage. After Hurricane Fran rolled through in 1996, only 120 feet remained, and it took $750,000 to restore it.

Surf City Ocean Pier is a very productive fishing pier for several kinds of fish. In November 1980, Loch Gunter, of Sanford, North Carolina, landed fifty-two flounder using a bucktail and strip bait. Richie Mungo, fourteen, of Charlotte, North Carolina, caught a 126-pound tarpon, establishing a new pier record. In June 1982, Jim Sly of Richmond, Virginia, decked a 55-pound cobia.

In 1970, Larry Lee, from Four Oaks, North Carolina, decked a thirty-three-pound, eight-ounce jack crevalle, which established a new state

Surf City Pier in the early '90s before it had to be rebuilt due to Hurricanes Bertha and Fran. *Courtesy of Missiles and More Museum.*

record. The current record is now a forty-seven-pound jack caught in 1989 off Cape Hatteras.

The popularity of the Surf City Ocean Pier is evident by its many loyal customers. Dan Bennett, from Wilmington, North Carolina, visits the Surf City Ocean Pier several times a year with his daughters. "That is where they have learned to cast an open face reel. Come to think of it that is where I learned also," Bennett recalls.

On July 4, 2009, the Surf City Ocean Pier conducted its first ever Children's Fishing Competition and Celebration. The event put 143 kids on the deck, free of charge, for a day of fishing, games, food and prizes. The experience exposed the kids to the fun and excitement of fishing in an educational environment.

The Surf City Ocean Pier sells bait and tackle and has a grill to feed hungry fishermen. It is located close to motels, restaurants and shops. The Surf City Ocean Pier also operates a website that keeps anglers and visitors updated on local events.

TRIPLE S FISHING PIER (1952–2006)

Atlantic Beach is one of the oldest vacation spots in North Carolina. By 1887, a small pavilion had been built on the island. The pavilion had a refreshment stand and a bathhouse where visitors could change clothes. Visitors were transported by sailboat to the eastern portion of Bogue Island. In 1916, the Atlantic View Beach Hotel was built on the site. Unfortunately, it was later destroyed in a fire.

In 1928, a toll bridge was built, and the tourist trade took off. Bathhouses and another beach resort with dining facilities, in addition to another pavilion, were built. Another hotel was also built, and in 1936 the toll bridge was turned over to the state, allowing the tolls to drop. In 1953, the toll bridge was replaced by a drawbridge, which was replaced in the 1980s with the current four-lane high-rise bridge.

The Triple S Pier was built in 1952 on the same site that had once been the location of a bathhouse and ballroom built in 1922 by V. Asbury in a section of Bogue Banks then known as Asbury Beach—later the town of Atlantic Beach.

The Triple S name came from the initials of its builder, S.S. Stevenson of Henderson, North Carolina. It was managed by Berry West, who would later manage the Iron Steamer and Bogue Inlet Piers. The Triple S Corporation eventually built a sixty-four-room motel, a 105-site campground and a mobile home park. In addition to the pier's tackle shop, the corporation operated a marina with fifty-five boat slips.

The Triple S was the closest pier to the Beaufort Inlet, which made it very productive. In 1978, a 105-pound amberjack was decked by angler Jack Long. Veteran angler Tony Stone, from Wilmington, North Carolina, got his start at the Triple S Pier

"I, along with siblings, cousins and friends, was taught how to fish by Granddaddy on the Triple S Pier," Stone said. "Through the years we have spent a lot of time at Sportsman's, Emerald Isle and the Iron Steamer piers." Like Stone, many anglers have a "home" pier, but they also often visit other piers, too.

In 1981, the Triple S Pier was purchased by Harry and Pat Rippy. They owned it, and were very popular with their customers, for twenty-five years. Then, in 2006, the pier was sold, quickly demolished and replaced by expensive beach cottages. Selling was "bittersweet," said Harry Rippy. He would not be the only one missing the pier,

"We've had a lot of good customers, a lot of faithful customers, a lot of people will hate to see it go. It's their pier, too," Rippy remarked to a reporter from the Raleigh *News and Observer.*

David Duke from Franklinton, North Carolina, photographed the demolition. Duke said Triple S was his family's favorite. "I offered the guy doing the demolition $1,000 for the Triple S sign," Duke recalls. Unfortunately, the man would not sell it.

Now with only the Oceanana Pier left at the far end of Atlantic Beach, many anglers are worried about the future of pier fishing in Carteret County. Jamie Barbor from Newport, North Carolina, who got his first fishing lesson on the Triple S Pier from his grandfather, says, "There is going to be no place to park or no place for the weary pier fisherman to rest his head." Barbor says, "Now I look at the Oceanana and say 'God, Save the Queen.'"

When the condos were built, the public lost not only a beloved fishing spot but also access to the beach itself. Triple S Pier had a parking lot that would accommodate over one hundred cars, and although the pier would charge a fee for parking, this space provided easy access to the beach. That, too, was lost when the pier was taken down.

KITTY HAWK FISHING PIER (1953–2003)

The northernmost fishing pier in the state, when it was built in 1953 the Kitty Hawk Pier was the third pier on the Outer Banks. The *1957 North Carolina Coastal Fishing and Vacation Guide* sums up local pier fishing: "Generally speaking one of the best bets for the angler who wants to catch a lot of fish is to hit the piers when the big run of blues, whiting and other close-to-the-shore species are running. For a couple of dollars or so, people can rent tackle, buy their bait and pay for the tariff for fishing privileges."

While inflation has driven costs of fishing well beyond the few dollars required in the 1950s, pier fishing is still a bargain compared to other types of fishing. Pier fishing is the easiest way to get the most out of your fishing trip; depending on the season and the migration patterns of the fish, piers can offer a good vantage point to get into the action.

Because Kitty Hawk Fishing Pier is the closest pier to the Chesapeake Bay, it has the advantage of catching migratory fish that move in and out of the huge bay. In the late 1960s, Kitty Hawk Fishing Pier held the record for

Ice on the pier at Kitty Hawk. The Kitty Hawk Pier is located the farthest north of all the piers in the state. *Courtesy of the Outer Banks History Center, Aycock Brown, photographer.*

Joe Menzacco (right) of Point Harbor, North Carolina, and his fishing partner with a nice haul of bluefish taken at the Kitty Hawk Pier. *Courtesy of the Outer Banks History Center, Aycock Brown, photographer.*

striped bass and bluefish. In 1982, a three-hundred-pound gray shark was landed by the same angler who had caught a fifty-four-pound cobia a short time before.

Chris Boyles from High Point, North Carolina, has fished fourteen of North Carolina's piers. He recalls a day in August during the early 1980s when twenty-seven kings were decked on the Kitty Hawk Pier. "The first two were decked before a dog day sunrise that promised to be a real scorcher in more ways than one," Boyles remembers. "The snakes [slang for king mackerel] were in thicker than fleas, and there was not a bluefish to be had for bait. The live bait was scarce, and I witnessed things I had never seen before, such as a live spot selling for ten bucks cash and a king hitting a trolley line that was baited with a dead spot."

The pier has had many owners over the years, including oil tycoon, philanthropist, power broker and UNC donor Walter Davis. (The undergraduate library in Chapel Hill bears his name.) In his book *The Walter*

The Golden Era of Pier Construction

Davis Story, biographer Ned Cline tells the story of Davis purchasing the Kitty Hawk Fishing Pier for $96,000. According to the story, the purchase was made after Davis complained to the pier's owner/manager, a man named Morgan, about the lack of Orange Crush soda in the vending machines. Morgan told him that if Davis didn't like the drink selection he should buy the pier and run it his way. He did and kept Morgan on as manager with instructions to keep plenty of Orange Crush in stock.

Davis owned the pier for over a decade before selling it for $2.5 million. According to his biography, when Davis sold the pier he gave half of the profits to the daughter of Ed Hurdle, his pier manager who was killed in an automobile crash, and divided the rest up among the remaining pier employees. Davis did not keep any of the profits for himself.

In the 1980s, the pier was owned by Dr. E.A. Murden Jr. of Portsmouth, Virginia. Today, the Kitty Hawk Fishing Pier is the property of the Hilton Gardens Hotel. Since the late 1990s, a hotel had been planned to be built on the site, but the on-again, off-again project was not realized in 2006.

The piers on the Outer Banks were mainly spared the fury of Hurricane Fran in 1996. But in September 2003 it would be their turn with Hurricane Isabel, a powerful storm that ripped a new inlet between Hatteras and Frisco and damaged property all over the Outer Banks. Isabel was especially damaging to fishing piers—all five of the piers on the northern banks suffered damage. But the timing was especially bad for the Kitty Hawk Pier, which had just undergone $300,000 in renovations.

At the time, the land on which the Kitty Hawk Fishing Pier was built was owned by a development company in Virginia that had purchased insurance on its investment. Most piers are typically not insured; it's simply too expensive, as the cost of the annual premium is equal to the profits that the pier makes in a year. This makes owning a pier about the riskiest venture a person can undertake. If the pier does have insurance, it's usually only for the part of the pier that is not over water.

But in the Kitty Hawk case, the development company had paid $85,000 for a $1,000,000 policy with a $250,000 deductible. After Isabel, the cost to rebuild was estimated at $1.6 million. The company chose not to rebuild the pier. Having just spent $300,000 on repairs, they lost their enthusiasm for the fishing business.

For five years, the shell of the pier house, and the remaining 220 feet of the pier, lay vacant. In 2006, after the Hilton Gardens Hotel was built on the site of the pier house, what remained of the pier was repaired and reopened in 2008. While it is a public pier, you must surrender a picture ID to be on the property if you are not staying at the upscale hotel.

Emerald Isle Pier (1954–1996)

Earl Thompson built the second pier on the Crystal Coast, this time on the western part of the Bogue Banks. Thompson began construction of his pier before the road was completed, and he had to truck the building materials to the pier using an old surplus marine half-track. The pier used steel for the pilings, and when it opened up in 1954, Thompson's Steel Pier featured a covered end to protect fishermen from the elements.

The pier was completed just in time to welcome Hurricane Hazel, which proceeded to damage the end of the pier and removed the covering that was there. For years, Thompson's Pier was known as being located where the pavement ends. Thompson sold the pier to three men: George Spell, J.A. Singleton and Bruce Shell. Ken Heverly, who had managed the pier prior to buying it, purchased the pier later. The name was changed to Emerald Isle Pier in 1961.

In its early years the Emerald Isle Pier was long, isolated and very productive. Otis Gardner fished there as a kid and spent many nights out on

Thompson's Steel Pier in the late 1950s. Anglers and visitors were grateful for the dedication of Earl and Doris Thompson, who had the foresight to build the pier even before there was a road. *Courtesy of Doris Lancaster Thompson, special thanks to Wayne and Kurt Thompson.*

the planks. According to Gardner, "On weekends they would have dances at the pavilion there. My parents were strict, and I was not allowed out at night with the exception of fishing, so I would bait up, go dancing and then bait up again then dance some more."

For a period of time, the Emerald Isle Pier held the women's state record for flounder and tarpon. In 1988, eighty-year-old Tony Moore caught a 103-pound cobia there. It would stand as a state record for twenty-three years.

The Emerald Isle Pier stood until 1996, when it succumbed during the summer of Bertha and Fran. Scott Edwards, from Castalia, North Carolina, used to make the 120-mile drive at night after work just to walk on the pier and then drive back. "I was sad when we lost that pier, it was my favorite," he recalls. Signs from the long-gone pier can be viewed at Flipperz Family Bar and Grill in Emerald Isle.

Today, like Jennette's Pier in Nags Head, the Emerald Isle Pier property is owned by the North Carolina Aquariums, and a concrete aquarium pier is planned for the future. The $15 to $20 million pier will be 750 feet long with an attached pier house, which will have a tackle shop, snack bar and educational exhibits. Wind-powered turbines for co-generating power, a geothermal well, a rainwater collection system and a gray water septic system are being considered for the pier. The land was donated by the Town of Emerald Isle, and if for any reason the pier is not built, the land will go back to the town.

JOLLY ROGER PIER (1954–   )

Lewis Orr built the Jolly Roger Pier in 1954, and in an interview captured in the 1993 documentary film *An Oral History of Topsail Beach*, Orr claimed to have gotten the idea from the newly constructed Surf City Pier. "They were making so much money I couldn't stand it," Orr said. "So I wanted to build something here." Giving his pier the name New Topsail Ocean Fishing Pier, he built it just to the right of the launching pad that was left over from the military's Project Bumblebee.

Topsail's twenty-six miles of perfect beaches had been in the hands of the military until a few years after the war ended. In the early 1950s, it was poised to be discovered by tourists and fishermen. Wilmington businessman Edgar Yow developed the central part of the island. A developer from Florida, J.G. "Slim" Anderson, bought the south end of the island, from sound to sea, and he promoted Topsail as the "Big Fish Capital of the World."

The new Topsail Ocean Pier was built right beside the launching pad for the navy's Project Bumblebee to develop and test the ramjet missile. The launching pad became the patio for the motel. *Courtesy of Missiles and More Museum.*

Lewis Orr's pier was only open a few months when it was destroyed by Hurricane Hazel. He started to rebuild almost immediately and reopened in 1955. The pier was 700 feet long. In 1960, the pier was extended out another 300 feet, making it over 1,000 feet in length. He purchased the skating rink to the left of the pier and converted it to a motel. Invoking Topsail's pirate ship past, he named it the Jolly Roger Motel. The old launching pad was left intact and serves as the patio for the motel. The name of the pier was officially changed to match the motel in the early 1970s, and the current length of the pier is about 850 feet.

The town of Topsail Beach was finally created in 1963, and Lewis Orr was the first mayor. The town has always strived to maintain its reputation as a family-friendly beach. And it is fisherman-friendly as well. In fact, the Jolly Roger Pier is the habitat of one of the coast's truly legendary fishermen. Certainly if any pier angler deserves the title of legendary, it is Topsail Beach's Angelo DePaola. "Deep" or "Deepy," as he's known by his countless friends, began fishing on the Jolly Roger soon after it opened in 1954. He

Lewis Orr Sr. observing the action at the Jolly Roger. *Courtesy of Missiles and More Museum.*

celebrated his eighty-eighth birthday in 2009, a year that started off slow for fishing on the North Carolina coast, especially for the big fish DePaola has made a passion of pursuing.

On one particular hot Saturday afternoon in June, on the end of the Jolly Roger Pier, there wasn't much going on. Anglers were sitting quietly on a bench. Suddenly, one of the fighting rods went off, and everyone sprung to attention.

The owner of the lucky rod looked down and checked his watch and then quickly made his way to his fishing rod, and the fight was on. The fish moved the angler to the center of the Jolly Roger Pier before taking him back again to the right corner. Skillfully, the angler worked the fish toward the pier under other anchor and fighting rods, and at one point the man climbed up the rail to give him more clearance to fight the fish. As he got the fish to the pier, it was spotted. "Shark," one of the other fishermen said, and indeed it was. The man fighting the shark worked him to the side of the pier, and someone helping him lowered the drop net to the hooked fish below. The shark once again shook his head, and the hook was dislodged, giving the angler an easy release.

That shark was far from memorable, as it was not a coveted king mackerel, but it was a chance to see a legend in action, bringing on more big fish to the side of the Jolly Roger Pier.

DePaola immigrated to Paterson, New Jersey, from Italy in 1928 with his family when he was eight years old. He joined the U.S. Marines in 1942 and served in Guam, Guadalcanal and Okinawa during World War II. He was stationed at Camp Lejeune and retired from the marines in 1946. Deciding to stay in the area, he took a job as a civilian employee at the base and eventually became the base's fire chief.

During his fifty-plus years of fishing on the Jolly Roger, DePaola became a king mackerel specialist. In 2007, he decked his 500th king—and it's no fish story. "Deep" has the records to prove it. DePaola has inspired other fishermen, such as Luther Dishman, from Southport, North Carolina, who now fishes the piers on Oak Island. Dishman recalls, "I fished with Deep off the Jolly Roger Pier in the early '70s. He was the 'man' back then, and I learned a lot just by watching and listening. I started my fishing log book because Deep had one."

DePaola also has a number of other remarkable catches, including a 112-pound tarpon, a 400-pound lemon shark and a 42-pound, seven-foot sailfish caught in 1978, a rarity from a pier. DePaola caught over forty kings in 1979 and followed this up by catching thirty in 1980. He once caught five kings in a single day.

Dishman also recalls that, in the early 1970s, there was a restaurant called Thompson's Restaurant across the street from the Jolly Roger Pier. This restaurant would cook your catch and "add coleslaw, hush puppies and tea for $1.25." Just a block north of the Jolly Roger Pier was Warren's Soda Shop, a popular hangout in Topsail Beach. Warren's is now called the Beach Shop and Grill.

Angelo DePaola with a couple of large red drum caught on the Jolly Roger. DePaola has recorded over five hundred king mackerel from the pier and is still going strong. *Courtesy of Bill Morris.*

When Dr. Earl Rubwright of Jacksonville, Florida, landed a tarpon on the pier, the Jolly Roger Pier became one of the first piers to catch a silver king. Large blues, drums, cobia and amberjacks have also been decked on the pier, along with kings and tarpons. Like all piers, the Jolly Roger Pier is popular in spot season and is excellent for Spanish mackerel and bluefish on plugs.

The Jolly Roger Pier has always had its fair share of

spectacular catches. A picture in the *Jacksonville Daily News* from May 31, 1972, perhaps shows it best. The photograph is of four anglers, all posing with their catches: Barry Huneycutt held a twenty-three-pound cobia; to the right of him Gerald Carbone presented his forty-five-pound cobia; to his right Luther Dishman held a five-pound, nine-ounce bluefish and a twenty-two-pound, three-ounce king; and to his right was Angelo's son Andy DePaola with a seventeen-pound, seven-ounce king.

In May 1981, the tackle shop and restaurant were destroyed in an early morning fire. The fire was discovered by a fisherman from Virginia who was sleeping in his car. The blaze was quickly under control. Despite the loss of the pier house, the Jolly Roger Pier remained open. The day of the fire, two kings were caught from the pier.

Lewis Orr Sr. passed away in 2005, but the pier is still in the Orr family. The Jolly Roger Pier and the motel are now owned by his sons Robin and Lewis Jr. and their sister, Teresa. The pier is open all year (weather permitting) and features a tackle store and a grill.

OAK ISLAND PIER (1955–   )

Oak Island is a fourteen-mile-long barrier island that runs east–west with a beach facing south, into the ocean. On the east side is the mouth of the Cape Fear River, on the west side is Lockwood's Folly Inlet. Oak Island has been inhabited since the early 1800s, and in 1836, Fort Caswell was erected on its far east end to guard the Cape Fear River and Wilmington, North Carolina, from attack. During the Civil War, when the fort was in Confederate hands, the Union army came up with plan after plan to attack, but the fortress seemed impenetrable. Instead, the Union attacked Fort Fisher, on the other side of Cape Fear. In the late 1940s, the abandoned fort was purchased by the Baptist State Convention of North Carolina and is used as a year-round retreat and conference center.

Just after you cross over the bridge to Oak Island from the mainland, there is a historical marker that reads: "Hurricane Hazel—Category 4 storm made landfall at Long Beach, October 15, 1954 with winds over 140 mph & 17-foot surge. Nineteen people killed in N.C." Up until 1999, when Hurricane Floyd killed fifty-six victims with its five-hundred-year flood, Hazel would be the storm against which people would measure and judge other hurricanes.

Hazel was indeed a hurricane for the ages. Here are some statistics for North Carolina alone:

- estimated $136 million in property damage (in 1954 dollars)
- nineteen deaths
- two hundred injuries
- fifteen thousand homes and structures destroyed
- thirty-nine thousand structures damaged

Included in that structure total are six coastal fishing piers destroyed and one damaged.

Oak Island's population was centered in two areas: Yaupon Beach to the east and Long Beach to the west. At the time of Hurricane Hazel, there were 357 buildings on Long Beach. After the storm, only 5 remained. Despite the near complete destruction of the island, residents were not deterred from rebuilding, and in 1955, the towns of Long Beach and Yaupon Beach were incorporated. In 1999, they merged to form the town of Oak Island.

Long Beach in the late 1940s was barely populated. After Hazel, it was the Yaupon Pier and the Long Beach Pier that helped bring visitors who would repopulate the island. *Courtesy of the North Carolina State Archives.*

The Golden Era of Pier Construction

The opening of Yaupon Pier (today's Oak Island Pier) in 1955 was a major part of the rebuilding effort after Hazel. It suffered its share of storm damage over the years, but then came Hugo in 1989, and Yaupon Pier was closed for the next four years—all but the three hundred feet nearest the pier house a "total loss." The owner, Peter Outlaw, came up with the idea of rebuilding with donor-sponsored planks, so for $10 you could buy a board that would go into the new deck. At that time, Outlaw estimated the cost at about $120,000. When the pier was finally complete in 1993, it was twenty-six feet above sea level, making it the tallest pier in the state.

Yaupon Pier has had its share of fishing memories. Buster Gunn, of Fayetteville, North Carolina, caught the first tarpon on the pier in 1978, a forty-nine-pounder. Yaupon Pier has also netted a forty-seven-pound African pompano and a thirty-eight-pound crevalle jack. The largest king decked at the pier was by Chuck Huthmacher, from Wilmington, North Carolina, who caught a fifty-pound king on April 15, 2002.

Like all of the piers on Oak Island, Yaupon Pier has a great place for king fishing. The best year in recent memories for king fishing in the entire state was 2007, and Yaupon led all piers with 244 kings decked.

Yaupon Pier's most famous fish was caught in 1966—a state record tiger shark caught by Walter Maxwell from Charlotte. The monster shark weighed 1,150 pounds and still holds the record. Maxwell was no stranger to record tiger sharks, as two years earlier he caught an even bigger one at Cherry Grove Pier in North Myrtle Beach, a giant that tipped the scales at 1,780 pounds and claimed him the world record.

Yaupon Pier has had a variety of owners over the years. In the early 1960s, it was owned by G.V. Barbee Jr. In the late 1980s and into the '90s, it was owned by the Outlaw family, and then Roy Fowler owned it for a while. A few years ago it became part of Cape Fear Trading Groups, which bought a number of properties on Oak Island and the surrounding area. A dispute erupted between the owners of the company, and soon the properties, including the pier, were put up for sale.

No buyer was found, and eventually Cape Fear Trading Groups went bankrupt. Cooperative Bank held the note and tried to sell Yaupon Pier at auction. Unfortunately, there were no bidders. Cooperative Bank closed the pier and boarded it up at the end of the 2007 fishing season.

An attempt by the Town of Oak Island to purchase the pier was voted down by the town council. Whether the town should go into the pier business remained a point of controversy through 2008, and the pier remained closed. People crowded the town meetings and voiced their opinions.

Yaupon Pier reopened as the Oak Island Pier in May 2009. The pier is now owned by the town and leased to Tommy Thomes, former owner of Long Beach Pier. *Photo by Al Baird.*

Concerns were that the town was overextending itself, or that Yaupon Pier would have an unfair advantage over the nearby Ocean Crest Pier. Supporters cited the loss of business from visitors that the pier brought in and the loss of even more public access. In August 2008, the North Carolina Public Access Foundation, a nonprofit organization dedicated to preserving access to North Carolina's public waterways, hooked up with fishermen from Yaupon and held a surf fishing tournament at the far west access of the island. Over fifty fishermen and over one hundred attendees showed up to show support for Yaupon Pier.

Armed with two state grants that totaled $800,000 and a new town council, Oak Island made a bid of $1.6 million for the pier. The offer was accepted by the bank in early 2009. The town found Tommy Thomes, the former owner of Long Beach Pier, to lease and operate what would be renamed Oak Island Pier. It reopened on May 11, 2009, and while the debate continues, fishermen who use the pier are relieved. The Oak Island Pier has become the first public pier in the state of North Carolina.

Business seems to have quickly returned; 250 season passes were sold in 2009, and Thomes has marketed the Oak Island Pier via newspapers across the state, as well as online and on social networking sites such as Facebook and MySpace.

Long Beach Pier (1956–2005)

It was like a wake, except people were dressed differently. December 31, 2005, was the last day Long Beach Pier was open. There was only one fisherman on the pier, and he wasn't catching anything. People were coming out and peering over the side or looking out at the horizon or back at the beach, trying to spot a familiar landmark. Some were taking pictures, and others were unbolting benches that they had purchased for twenty dollars apiece.

The pier house was packed. People were getting bargains and mementos from the landmark that had been a fixture on Oak Island since 1956. Due to the divorce of the pier's owner, the Long Beach Pier and the motel were being sold. The land would be divided up into ten lots, some of them bringing in $1 million. The Long Beach Pier went out with a bang, hosting a New Year's Eve party complete with fireworks, live music and a bonfire on its last night in business.

Carolyn Riggaw, who had been a regular at Long Beach Pier until it was closed in 2005 and then torn down in 2006, says with a smile, "You always remember your first king," as she stood with other anglers at the end of the Oak Island Pier. Her first king had been a twenty-three-pound fish, taken in

This picture was taken on December 31, 2005, the last day the pier was opened for business. *Photo by Al Baird.*

at the Long Beach Pier. Brent Everidge, when talking with Riggaw, agreed that you always remember your first and said his was a twenty-four-pounder caught on Yaupon Pier. "I caught it my first day king fishing," he laughs. "I thought to myself, this is easy!"

Both anglers then turned to Luther Dishman. Dishman had started fishing at Topsail Pier and on the Jolly Roger Pier and then, after moving to Southport, North Carolina, fished the Long Beach Pier in the 1970s. Dishman then took a fifteen-year break from pier fishing, opting instead to fish for kings from his boat. He returned to pier fishing in 2007, when he began fishing from Yaupon Pier. When the two anglers asked him what was his first, he just smiled and says, "I don't remember."

The Long Beach Pier was originally built by Jimmy Bigford in 1955. He later sold it to Harvey Ratcliffe. The pier was then owned by Jimmy Ratcliffe before it was sold to Dave Beckner in the late 1980s. In 1998, the pier was sold to Tommy Thomes, a developer who built homes on Oak Island for many years.

The Long Beach Pier was long, over one thousand feet, and the closest to the inlet at Lockwood's Folly. Famous for its king mackerel fishing, it also had enough amenities to provide fun for any vacation. With two motels on site, a campground, grocery, tackle store, grill and gift shop, a trip to the pier could last a day or a couple of weeks. The Long Beach Pier structure was an attraction in and of itself. Not only was the pier long, but it also had an observation deck at the end that could be used for sightseeing or fish spotting.

If there was a king of king mackerel fishing piers in North Carolina, it was likely Long Beach Pier. In May 1978, it decked 219 kings in a seven-day span, with 56 caught on May 22 and 44 on May 18. Luther Dishman (who had learned king fishing from the legendary Angelo DePaola at Topsail) was fishing the pier during this time, and his log book shows that he caught 10 kings during this single week. Dishman's kings ranged from fifteen to twenty-six pounds. The last one he caught on a dead bluefish, as there were no more live baits to be had.

"I would show up after work and just try and catch one," Dishman says. "Looking back on it now, I should have taken a couple days off from work." Asked if he ever thought there would be a time when the really good fishing would come to an end, he quietly says, "It never crossed my mind."

Ed Potter, from Wilmington, North Carolina, recalls the day he caught an eighty-pound cobia while fishing for kings at the pier. "I had on a two-pound bluefish and forty-pound test line, and that darn fish nearly spooled me that day," Potter says. "That was one fine pier."

Katherine Davis of Long Beach caught a fifty-three-pound, three-ounce king on the Long Beach Pier in May 1991. She fought the fish for forty-five minutes before it was gaffed. Davis accomplished this amazing feat on sixteen-pound test line and was awarded the official line class record for a woman by the International Game Fish Association (IGFA).

In 1999, some catches of note were made. First, in May of that year, David Dyson of Greensboro, North Carolina, caught a sixty-eight-pound cobia off the end of the Long Beach Pier. Then, in the first week of July, a pair of local anglers, Freddy Williams and Pat Berry, landed a thirteen-pound, two-ounce bluefish and a ten-pound, two-ounce sheepshead, respectively.

The financial storm of rising real estate values eventually made the Long Beach Pier and motel more valuable as oceanfront housing than as a business. In a story in the *Wilmington Star*, owner Tommy Thomes was quoted as saying, "Our city and our county are growing. You can't stand in the way of progress. You'll just get run over. I would like to see Oak Island stay a small beach town, but those days are over, and life must go on."

Ironically, since the pier was sold, the price of real estate has fallen. The end result is the ten vacant beachfront lots in a spot that entertained generations of happy tourists and fishermen alike.

Center Fishing Pier (1956–1996)

In 1956, Center Pier became the third pier on Pleasure Island. It was built in Wilmington Beach, a small unincorporated community located between Carolina Beach and Kure Beach. The pier originally was known as Winner Pier, after the family who built it, but soon became known as Center or Central Pier because of its location on the barrier island.

Walter Winner built the Fort Fisher Pier in 1936 and began building the Center Pier in 1956 for J.C. Bame, owner of the Bame Hotel. In the early 1960s, the pier was owned by C.W. Snead and was operated, along with the attached restaurant, by Bob Manning. Manning and his wife also owned and operated the Manning Motel, which was located across the street from the Center Pier.

In 1957, the Carolina Beach Chamber of Commerce was advertising the area as a "year 'round seaside city" with four ocean fishing piers on five miles of coast.

In the mid-1960s, the Center Pier was owned by James and Doris Herring. Doris Herring was part of the Bame family, who owned Fisherman's Steel Pier in Carolina Beach. The Herrings owned the pier for more than thirty years before deciding not to rebuild it after the storms of 1996.

Jack Wood from Marion, North Carolina, is a lifelong pier fishing enthusiast. He was hooked on his very first trip to the Center Pier, when he was twelve years old. He made the three-hundred-mile trip to the coast with his mother, his sister, Gale, and his brother-in-law, Ray. The next year, 1963, he convinced his dad to make the trip. His dad set the hook on his first bluefish, and when he finally got the four-pounder to the deck, he also became a dedicated pier fisherman.

Wood remembers those early days at the Center Pier: "Mrs. Manning operated the pier house restaurant and, with her husband, kept the motel going."

Center Pier caught its share of fish. In 1988, Max Weavil caught a sixty-two-pound cobia and Jeff Grier decked a seventy-two-pound amberjack. Center Pier also laid claim to a ninety-pound tarpon that was caught in the mid-1980s. Jimmy Sellers of Wilmington caught a forty-three-pound king at Center Pier in 1981.

Center Pier nearly closed to public fishing in 1984, when a company called the Boardwalk Development Company decided to build a large condominium called the Ocean Gate Inn. A presale advertisement boasted, "Ocean Gate Inn residents will enjoy their own ocean fishing pier," and individual units were starting at a mere $69,900.

The Center Pier can be seen in the background as vacationers enjoy the surf and sand at Carolina Beach in 1983. The pier was part of many plans that never materialized. Now it is featured as the Tiki Bar at the Golden Sands Motel. *Courtesy of New Hanover Public Library,* Star-News *Archives.*

A softening in the real estate market the following year caused a number of initial investors to back out, and by 1985, the Ocean Gate Inn project was in jeopardy. Then, James Pope, owner of the Golden Sands Motel next door to the proposed project, got permission to expand his motel to part of the lot where Ocean Gate Inn was to be built in the fall of 1985. The project was now basically cancelled. Center Pier would remain a public pier.

In May 1986, the Boardwalk Development Company filed for Chapter 11 bankruptcy. The lawyer for the project and one of the original investors, David Rock Whitten, were accused of embezzlement. David Rock Whitten fled the country after faking his own drowning by leaving his boat idling at Snow's Cut Channel between the Cape Fear River and Wrightsville. The next day, he was spotted at Myrtle Beach Airport, en route to Guatemala. He got as far as Mexico before turning around and returning to the States. He pled guilty and got a ten-year sentence.

Center Pier battled the usual big name storms that other piers in the area had to cope with. Center Pier was completely destroyed by Hurricane Hazel and, while it was being rebuilt, lost 150 feet to Hurricane Hugo in 1989. When Hurricanes Bertha and Fran came calling in 1996, the Herring family decided not to rebuild Center Pier.

Today, you can walk out onto the remains of the Center Pier that extend into the surf. There are three pilings sticking out of the water where the end of the pier would have been. Although you can't fish on the pier, you can have a drink and something to eat at the Ocean Mist's Tiki Bar, which is located on the deck of the old pier.

From the vantage point of the Tiki Bar, you can see Kure Pier to the south and Carolina Beach Pier to the north. This area is popular with surfers, and the elevated deck offers a great place to catch the action as they hang ten.

The Golden Sands now has two large five-story motel buildings where the pier's parking lot once stood. Every room has a view of the ocean and what little remains of the Center Pier.

SPORTSMAN'S PIER (1956–2006)

On the day it closed—October 28, 2006—the sign at the entrance of the Sportsman's Pier on Atlantic Beach still read, "Sportsman's Pier, You Should Have Been Here Yesterday." The words rang with bitter irony as people—many of them longtime devotees of Sportsman's—were bidding on everything from lighting fixtures to fishing tackle. Owner David Bradley was even there

Power lines being repaired shortly after Finch's Ocean Pier was built. A short time later, the pier was called Sportsman's Pier, and the name stuck. *Courtesy of the North Carolina State Archives.*

to autograph signs and other memorabilia. The boom in real estate values had finally induced him to sell the pier that had been in his family since 1963.

Sportsman's Pier was built in 1956 on the part of Atlantic Beach that was once known as Money Island. Originally, Sportsman's Pier was known as Finch's Ocean Pier after its manager, Bill Finch. Later, it became Bill Finch's Sportsman's Pier before finally settling on the name Sportsman's Pier.

Sportsman's Pier had a full-service bait and tackle store, as well as a gift shop and restaurant. The restaurant was complete with a lounge and full-service ABC permits. The pier featured many benches and a covered deck from which to take in the action and stay out of the elements.

Sportsman's Pier was very popular and produced some nice catches over the years. Many of these were 40-pound-plus king mackerel, some 82- and 86-pound cobias, a 60-pound amberjack and 65- and 68-pound tarpon. One of the most incredible days the pier had was in 1967, before shark fishing was banned on the pier. Eight huge sharks between 385 and 1,135 pounds were caught.

The Golden Era of Pier Construction

Sportsman's Pier was once over 1,100 feet long, but after Hurricanes David and Gloria it was reduced to about 950 feet.

In May 1977, there was a pier house fire that destroyed the pier house and a lot of the pier's records and photographs. There were twenty-four anglers on the pier when the fire started in the early hours of the morning, and all narrowly escaped injury by slipping out the side gate.

By late October 2006, Sportsman's Pier, which had put about 33,000 anglers and over 100,000 visitors a year out over the water, was no more. And the auction was on.

Anglers were, for the most part, getting good deals on the tackle, but the competitive fishermen often raised prices while engaged in bidding wars. In one particular instance, two anglers had bid the price of a rod and reel combo over fifteen dollars higher than the posted retail sign a few inches away. While these fishermen paid more than they would have in stores, these items were valued more as keepsakes than as fishing gear. Anything with the name Sportsman's Pier on it quickly became in demand.

Signs from the pier were also popular. Just outside the pier house, owner David Bradley was autographing many of the signs for the purchasers. Bradley looked melancholy as he signed and dated the signs. When one autograph seeker looked at him and said, "This must be hard for you," he simply nodded and said, "It is."

Sportsman's Pier was in the Bradley family for decades. Bradley's dad, Ken, purchased the pier with Bradley's uncle, Chester Pittman, and the two started running the pier in 1963. Five years later, the elder Bradley bought out Pittman and became the sole owner of the pier. Over the last several years, coastal land values exploded, raising property taxes and insurance costs. These costs continued to rise and, paired with the ever pending threat of hurricanes taking out the entire investment, played an important part in David Bradley's decision to sell the pier.

Anglers and vacationers were also upset about losing the Sportsman's Pier. Kris Pritchett from Onslow, Massachusetts, first vacationed at Atlantic Beach as a kid with his family in the 1970s and 1980s. Pritchett remembers, "Since my dad loved to fish we always stayed at a place near the pier." He started going back in 2000, and news that Sportsman's Pier closed hit the family hard. "My kids will be devastated over losing Sportsman's," he says. "They loved the big outside saltwater tanks as well as eating breakfast out on the pier."

Doug Leister attempted to have the state purchase Sportsman's Pier and keep it in operation. He started an online petition and got widespread support from the fishing and beachgoing public, but no state agency came to help. One of Leister's fellow fishermen, Charlie Mullins of Morehead City, wrote a moving letter published in that city's *News-Times*. It included the following: "In my will, I have requested that my body be cremated and my ashes be scattered off the end of Sportsman's Pier. Looks like that is one wish I will not be granted. I have had the satisfying experience to observe the spreading of the ashes of two of my friends from the pier."

FISHERMAN'S STEEL PIER (1956–1977)

If there was ever a pier that deserved the disclaimer "It seemed like a good idea at that time," it would be Fisherman's Steel Pier on Carolina Beach. J.R. Bame and his son, J.C. Bame, both Carolina Beach businessmen, were approached with the idea to build a steel pier in 1955. The elder Bame, who already owned a hotel and Center Pier, thought it was a good idea. So, in 1955, they began construction on the state's third steel pier. The price tag was estimated at about $75,000. At the very beginning of construction,

In 1945, Carolina Beach did not have a fishing pier. Eleven years later, the town featured three. Fisherman's Steel Pier was constructed at the end of the boardwalk near the amusement park. *Courtesy of the North Carolina State Archives.*

Hurricane Connie destroyed half of what had been built, but the pier was operational by 1956.

Angler Jack Wood recalls the location of Fisherman's Steel Pier as "downtown at the boardwalk. The entrance was behind the bumper cars and north of the putt-putt." That put it right across the street from Carolina Beach's largest amusement park, Seashore Park. The pier was built on the site of the Fergus cottage, which was destroyed by Hurricane Hazel, and R.C. Fergus would later become part owner. The one-thousand-foot-long pier was an instant attraction, but—as was the case with other steel piers in the state—the metal did not hold up in the salt water.

Fisherman's Steel Pier had an arcade and a grill, but the main feature was the Skyliner chairlift, which lifted sightseers thirty feet into the air and out over the length of the pier. Many old postcards of the pier and the ride can be found online or in antique stores.

In the late 1960s, Bame and Fergus sold Fisherman's Steel Pier to Effie and Howard McGirt from Zebulon, North Carolina, who were looking for something to do during their retirement years at the beach. One common postcard from 1970 shows the McGirts standing in front of the Skyliner ride at the entrance of the pier.

The pier lost about 150 feet to a storm in 1969, and by the early 1970s, the pier was too much upkeep for the McGirts, who returned it to Bame and Fergus. Fisherman's Steel Pier was closed and demolished shortly after. In 1978, a shorter pier (40 feet) was planned on that location, but by then the fame that the Carolina Beach boardwalk had enjoyed in the '50's and '60s was starting to decline. Speaking of Fisherman's Steel Pier, R.C. Bame later said to the *Wilmington Star News*, "I would call it a failure."

However, it may be reborn yet again—this time as a concrete structure. The Town of Carolina Beach has purchased the land near where the pier once stood and is partnering with the North Carolina Aquariums with a plan to build the third of the aquarium concrete piers there. (The first, Jennette's, is in Nags Head, with a second planned for Emerald Isle.) Carolina Beach and the aquariums have also discussed bringing back an attraction similar to the old Skyliner.

OCEAN ISLE PIER (1957–   )

On just about any day on any pier in North Carolina you can see an angler walking leisurely along the side of the pier, holding his rod over the water and slowly working his bait. One fall afternoon, two anglers were doing this at Ocean Isle Pier on Ocean Isle Beach. They had live finger mullets on a J-hook at the end of a leader. An egg-shaped sinker was on the line above the swivel, allowing the finger mullet a certain amount of freedom. The sandy, smooth bottom at Ocean Isle Pier makes it ideal for flounder fishing, which is what these anglers were doing. Outside of king fishermen, flounder fishermen are as patient as any angler can get.

Ocean Isle is a south-facing island, with Shallotte Inlet to the east and Tubbs Inlet to the west. During World War II, the Coast Guard had a station on Ocean Isle Beach and used a horse patrol at the station to spot German U-boats that were menacing the coast. In 1953, Odell Williamson, one of the most decorated veterans of the war, and Mannon Gore bought the entire seven-mile barrier island for $213,000. Williamson wanted to create a family vacation island, but after Hurricane Hazel only two of the seventeen houses were left. And more than houses were gone: Williamson lost his sister, brother-in-law and nephew in the storm. Despite the tragedy, Williamson immediately bought his partner Gore's share of the devastated island.

Williamson started to build Ocean Isle Pier in 1956, three years before the community was officially born. It was finished in 1957. Today there are still fewer than one thousand permanent residents of the island, but during tourist season the island swells with people.

In 1989, it would cost you three dollars a day for bottom fishing off the Ocean Isle Pier or eight dollars for king fishing. A season pass was forty-five dollars per person or seventy dollars for husband and wife.

The Ocean Isle Pier features a grill, arcade, gift shop and tackle and bait shop. The pier grill serves the only breakfast on Ocean Isle Beach.

BARNACLE BILL'S PIER (1957–1996)

A little north of the Surf City Pier, on Topsail Island, two pilings stand alone in the Atlantic Ocean. As the tide ebbs and flows, a closer look reveals a third piling broken off near the waterline. This is all that remains of Barnacle Bill's Pier.

Barnacle Bill's Pier was the second of five built in Surf City. Mike Scott remembers vacationing there with his parents when he was growing up: "Barnacle Bill's Fishing Pier was the hangout for me. I can remember if you were standing on Barnacle Bill's you could look to your left and see the Scotch Bonnet Pier and to your right you could see Surf City Fishing Pier. Beyond Scotch Bonnet you could also see the Ocean City Pier, which was considered the minority fishing pier back in the day."

The Golden Era of Pier Construction

The officers' club left over from the days of Camp Davis became Barnacle Bill's pier house. The pier itself was one thousand feet in length and featured a tackle shop, gift shop, game room and grill. Scott remembers that most piers had a grill, and if you caught a fish and cleaned it, they would cook it for you. Barnacle Bill's Pier also had facilities for campers and trailers.

Barnacle Bill's Pier was originally owned by Wilmington businessman E.A. Rusher and his partner, C.N. Traynahum. The pier was built in 1957 and sold to Charlie Medlin in 1966. The Medlin family operated the pier until it closed thirty years later. The Medlin family also owned the Paradise Pier, located three piers to the north.

Charles Venson Medlin was the son of a tobacco farmer from Nash County who, in 1952, moved to Surf City with his wife and son, Doug. Medlin became one of the island's first residents and business owners with a store called Coastal Company that sold ice and seafood. In 1958, before getting into the pier business, he opened Medlin's Grocery.

Doug Medlin also recalls what it was like at the piers in the mid-1960s and 1970s: "It was competitive between the piers but generally you had the same regular customers, the competition was to see which pier could do the best." The biggest challenge for the pier owners was to keep up with the repairs.

Barnacle Bill's Pier in the winter season would leave the gate open so local and regular fishermen could access the pier while it was closed. *Courtesy of Missiles and More Museum.*

"Even in the little storms there would be damage to the pier that needed to be attended to," he said.

The fact that Barnacle Bill's Pier was sandwiched between the other piers did not affect its production. The pier had a state record twenty-one-pound triple tail caught in 1967, along with an eighty-six-pound tarpon and a thirty-four-pound crevalle jack decked in 1977. Tim Kirkpatrick caught a sixty-seven-pound cobia in June 1980 off the pier.

Barnacle Bill's Pier produced a lot of good catches of a variety of fish. John Pendergrass of Rocky Mount, North Carolina, had a catch of 200 spot, 70 Virginia mullet and eight flounder in early June 1981. In early May 1978, Bobby Ferrell caught 207 spots and Virginia mullets in a day. Connie Halley caught a seven-pound sheepshead in August 1980.

In late July 1981, Robbie Morgan, ten, from Holly Ridge, North Carolina, landed a forty-pound amberjack that measured fifty inches long. He caught the fish on a live bluefish. The monster fish was bigger than the young fisherman.

Pier fishermen are often surprised at what they catch. It can vary from a species that is out of its typical season, to some strange-looking creature that you need to go to the books to identify, to other fish that are seldom if ever found inshore. Such was the case in 1984, when Jan Lancaster of LaGrange, North Carolina, and Noah Jones of Lewisville, North Carolina, caught identical fourteen-pound dolphin. Dolphin, or mahi-mahi as it is now known, are typically found in the Gulf Stream and not so close to the shore, but sometimes strong offshore currents or winds can bring them near land.

Seventy-five feet of the Barnacle Bill's Pier was destroyed by Hurricane Diana in 1984, causing over $100,000 worth of damage. The next year, Hurricane Gloria cut Barnacle Bill's in half. In 1989, Hurricane Hugo took out fifteen feet of the middle of the pier. The end came in 1996, when Hurricanes Bertha and Fran made their infamous one-two punch.

"We had just finished making the repairs [$75,000 worth] from Bertha when Fran came a-calling and took out the entire pier," Doug Medlin says, with a laugh. Instead of rebuilding, he threw in the towel and sold the land as ten oceanfront lots. At the time, a Century 21 realtor estimated their value at $800,000 *each*. Medlin still owns a tackle store in Surf City, East Coast Sports, which he expanded after closing his pier and selling the property.

Paradise Pier (1958–1985)

Topsail Island got another pier in 1958 when the Paradise Pier was built. Charlie Medlin, who already owned Barnacle Bill's Pier, bought the Paradise in 1963 and sold it in 1966.

Charlie's son Doug Medlin recalls what it was like operating two businesses at the beach in those days: "A major concern was getting enough labor to staff both piers and two restaurants during the vacation season."

In those days, Topsail Island piers, and many others on the coast, catered to farmers—mainly tobacco farmers—from eastern North Carolina. The vacation season usually started in spring, after the farmers got their crops into the field. "They would show up at the beach and stay until harvest time," Doug Medlin recalls. He also noted that they would not spend much money at this time. "It was rare to see a twenty-dollar bill," he says.

Families would start to arrive at the beach when school was done for the year. This helped incrementally increase the volume of business. However, the best business season at the beach was the fall, both for fishing and for profits.

In the fall, farmers would return to the beach in time for spot season. By now they had harvested and sold their tobacco crops, and as Medlin recalls, "They would buy everything in sight." While seeing a Jackson in the spring was rare, in the fall making change for a Franklin (fifty-dollar bill) was commonplace. Doug Medlin remembered his father saying that if your business was breaking even by Labor Day you were in first-class shape.

In those days the big attraction in the fall was the spot runs. "Why spots are popular," Medlin recalls, "is that anyone can catch them. All you have to do is drop a line over the side of the pier." Medlin says many people would just can them whole in Mason jars to preserve them.

Of course, big game fish were also caught at Paradise Pier, including 128- and 125-pound tarpon. In 1977, a monster 159-pound silver king was landed. In June 1982, Jim Osburn, of Hubert, North Carolina, caught a 66-pound cobia on live bait off the end of the Paradise Pier.

In 1964, Wayne Boys hooked into a tarpon on the Paradise Pier that ended up taking him down the beach. To bring the fish in, a much younger Doug Medlin swam out past the breakers with a gaff and hooked the fish behind its gills and then dragged it to the beach. A picture of Boys, Medlin and the tarpon made its way into the local papers.

The Paradise Pier went through various owners and operators after the Medlins. In 1984, it was owned by Stanley McCauley. In May of that year,

The strong north winds spread the fire on the Paradise Pier so fast that five anglers were trapped on the planks and had to escape by jumping into the water. *Courtesy of Missiles and More Museum.*

an electrical short in the tackle shop started a fire. The fire's flames were fanned by brisk north winds and spread rapidly. There were a couple dozen people on the pier at the time, and while most escaped easily, five people were trapped on the planks. To escape, they had to dive into the water, where they were rescued by three surfers and taken to shore.

Ironically, Doug Medlin was the Surf City fire chief at the time. He estimated damage to be about $1 million. People recalling the fire said that for a day or two after, when the charred pilings became exposed at low tide, they would start to smolder again.

The pier was not rebuilt, and in 1986, the land was rezoned for high-density housing.

OCEAN CITY FISHING PIER (1959–1996)

During the Jim Crow era of the segregated South, things were separate but not equal, and the coast was no exception. In the 1920s, there was a small location on Atlantic Beach that was designated for African Americans, but that didn't last long. After the Second World War, things began to transform, albeit very slowly. In North Carolina, not only were African Americans not welcomed at the beach, but some towns and communities even had laws on the books prohibiting selling them land.

In 1949, that changed when former Wilmington mayor and prominent lawyer Edgar Yow bought a six-mile stretch of Topsail Island and planned to develop it. One of the first communities he laid out was a one-mile stretch of beach located just north of Surf City. Yow, who was white, partnered with two prominent black families from Wilmington, the Chestnuts and the Grays, and formed the Ocean City resort. Rather than turning away African Americans, Yow and his partners welcomed them to this prime stretch of beach. Wade Chestnut managed the resort and promoted the new beachfront community to other black professionals.

After Hurricane Hazel, Ocean City had to be rebuilt, and it included a motel, dining hall, dormitory, chapel and, by 1959, the only fishing pier in North Carolina that was open to African Americans. Dewey Brown, fifty, recalls spending many summer nights hanging out at the Ocean City Pier. In an article written by *News and Observer* reporter Andrea Weigl, who covered Ocean City's sixtieth anniversary, Brown said, "We developed strong relationships with other families. It was really a home away from home."

The nine-hundred-foot pier was built at the site of one of the observation towers for Project Bumblebee. The tower, which in 1951 was known as the Ocean City Beach Terrace, was converted to a tackle shop and restaurant.

Like most of the piers on Topsail, the Ocean City Fishing Pier was destroyed in 1996 by Bertha and Fran and did not reopen. But several pilings and cross members still remain. The observation tower, though damaged, also remains. Locals still consider the location excellent for speckled trout.

George Tyson was the pier manager in the 1970s, and he often gave fishing reports in the Wilmington *Star*. Spots, trout, bluefish and kings were frequently in his reports. The Ocean City Fishing Pier was also known for excellent bottom fishing and as a good flounder spot. The pier also had its share of king mackerel, and in 1976, it landed a seventy-three-pound amberjack, one of the largest ever recorded in the state.

In 1993, an eighty-five-pound spinner shark was decked at the pier. Spinner sharks in North Carolina are at their northernmost point in their

An observation tower from Project Bumblebee became part of the pier house for the Ocean City Pier. *Courtesy of Missiles and More Museum.*

East Coast range, and while these sharks can get to two hundred pounds on the West Coast, an eighty-five-pound Atlantic spinner shark is an unusually large fish.

While it was the only African American pier in the days of segregation, the Ocean City Fishing Pier may have been the first pier to integrate. Terry Mosely remembers vacationing as a teenager at the Surf City Campground and walking to the Ocean City Pier with his cousins to play pool and drink beer for only thirty-five cents per can. "It would be years before I realized that Ocean City was a 'black pier,' and the guys behind the counter must have wondered what the heck we were doing there. In any case, we always felt welcomed as long as our money held out."

OUTER BANKS FISHING PIER (1959–)

On a sunny Monday morning in September 2009, an elderly angler made his way out over the Outer Banks Fishing Pier assisted by a taller man who, while carrying the gentleman's fishing rod and pulling his equipment and cooler, turned and asked politely, "Your usual spot?" The angler nodded, and his gear was moved another fifty feet down the pier and placed on a bench. His assistant—pier owner Garry Oliver—then walked back toward his pier house and sat at a picnic table under an umbrella. "That man I was helping is ninety-three years old. He is a Baptist preacher from just west of here, and he has been coming here since the '70s."

At sixty-three, Oliver is the dean of North Carolina pier owners, having owned and operated his pier since 1969. (That's right: he was twenty-three when he started.) Like many pier anglers, Oliver first came to the Outer Banks as a kid with his family on summer vacations. His father was a Washington lobbyist from Texas, and the family would spend three weeks at Nags Head every summer. Oliver's first pier experience was on the Nags Head Pier. When he thinks about the previous generation of pier owners, he talks about how "they raised me."

Oliver never intended to get into the pier business—he had his sights set on a political career. He was the vice-president of the Young Democrats from Texas and, in 1968, attended the party's convention in Chicago—best known for its week of rioting in the streets. "That whole experience disillusioned me about politics," Oliver said. "I started looking for something else to do." When he came back to Nags Head the next year, the pier was for sale, and he convinced his dad to loan him the money. At twenty-three, Garry Oliver became the owner of a Nags Head institution that he has nurtured for over forty years.

The original pier, known as the Seaport Fishing Pier, was built by West Virginia businessman Red Mitchell in 1959. Mitchell ran it until his death in 1968. The family continued to run the pier until they sold it to Oliver in 1969. Oliver changed the name to Outer Banks Fishing Pier.

And he made other changes, including opening his pier to African American customers. "We were one of the first to welcome blacks," Oliver said. "Some still remember that and thank me for doing it."

Like most piers, the Outer Banks Fishing Pier has a core group of anglers who call it their home pier. He is proud to say, "In some cases people have been coming here for five generations,"

Over the years, Oliver has noted the changes in the demographics of the people at the pier. "Saturdays used to be the busiest days, and during the summer every week there would be a group of ten to twelve boys that would spend their week at the beach here," he said. "Now they have other options." Oliver still thinks the fishing piers are the gateway to the next generation of sportsmen. "That is where I learned how to fish," he remembers.

Left: Large bluefish were frequently decked at the Seaport Fishing Pier in Nags Head. Oliver changed the name of the pier to the Outer Banks Fishing Pier when he bought it in 1969. *Courtesy of the Outer Banks History Center, Aycock Brown, photographer.*

Below: Garry Oliver (fourth from the left) and a group of Outer Banks Pier regulars hooked up with some trophy channel bass one evening in the 1970s. *Courtesy of Garry Oliver, Aycock Brown, photographer.*

Besides being a productive pier for bottom fishing and plugging, the Outer Banks Fishing Pier has done very well over the years with larger species. Kings, amberjacks and cobia all have been claimed off its deck. In 1992, a seventy-two-pound cobia was landed. The pier has seen its fair share of big blues and large red drum as well. In the late fall, if the water temperature drops low enough, the pier can be a good location to catch striped bass.

The pier is located at milepost 18.5 and is the southernmost of the Northern Banks piers. The pier sells tackle and bait and has a grill. Rental equipment is also available. Oliver also owns a tackle store, Fishing Unlimited, and a sound pier on the causeway to Manteo from which he rents boats.

After his pier took a beating during Hurricane Isabel in 2003, Oliver got creative. He raised money for rebuilding by having events like a pig picking and rummage sales and selling pier passes at a discount.

OCEANANA PIER (1959–)

A.B. Cooper, who helped develop the town of Atlantic Beach on Bogue Banks, gave the community its third fishing pier in 1959 when he erected the Oceanana Resort and Pier between the Triple S and Sportsman's Pier. Cooper had intended to call his business the Oceana Resort, but an overzealous sign painter added an extra "na" at the end. The resort featured a motel, playground, pool with a fountain and a private beach.

The Oceanana was originally over 1,200 feet long, and A.B. Cooper ran the resort and pier until his death in 2001. They are now owned by his son, Buddy Cooper.

On Mother's Day 1975, the pier decked fifty-two king mackerel. This is second to only Long Beach Pier for the most recorded kings in a single day. The Oceanana Pier also has rung up a seventy-six-pound cobia, a three-hundred-pound hammerhead shark, a sixty-two-pound amberjack and an eighteen-pound, four-ounce bluefish, an IGFA record on six-pound test line.

King fishing is no longer permitted on the pier, but Oceanana is a popular spot for pluggers. Warm October days find the end of the pier lined with anglers vying for bluefish or Spanish, and they are not disappointed.

The lures that the anglers are plugging with are Got-Cha plugs made by Sea Striker, a company located in Morehead City, just over the bridge from the pier. If you are on a pier and you do not see a Got-Cha plug, chances are you are not in North Carolina. The lures are popular because they catch fish— Spanish, bluefish, trout, pompano and even flounder are caught with them.

The Oceanana was located between the Triple S and Sportsman's Pier on Atlantic Beach. In 2006, the other piers were removed to make room for oceanfront housing; only the Oceanana remains. *Courtesy of the Carteret County Historical Society, Inc., Morehead City, North Carolina.*

After the Sportsman's and Triple S closed in 2006, the Oceanana Pier is the only pier remaining on the far end of Atlantic Beach and one of three left on Bogue Banks. It is flanked by the exclusive private Dunes Club on one side and by Cooper's mobile home park on the other. He is looking at options of turning his motel into a condotel, a condo building that rents the units out when the owners aren't using them.

Cooper is unsure of the future of the Oceanana Pier, as the new structure would tear down the motel and move the mobile home park to another location. Cooper told *Carteret News-Times* reporter Mike Shutak, "My dad put me to work at seven years old setting pins at a bowling alley. I haven't had a day off since and I am ready to retire and enjoy my autumn years."

BOGUE INLET PIER (1959–   )

Bogue Inlet Pier was built near the western end of Bogue Banks in 1959 by Bill McLean and George Spell. The pier was purchased by the Stanley family in 1971. Mike Stanley is the current owner of the pier and the campground also on the property.

Bogue Inlet Pier is the second longest pier over water in the state and features shaded benches and an observation deck at the end of the pier. *Photo by Al Baird.*

Bogue Inlet Pier is arguably one of the best maintained and equipped piers in the state. The current pier is one thousand feet long and features a restaurant and bait and tackle shop. Benches spaced in intervals located in the center of the pier are topped to provide shade and wind protection. Additional benches are located near the rails.

There is an observation deck located at the end of the pier that is ideal for sightseeing, fish spotting and taking in the excitement of the anglers who are king fishing. On one October afternoon, however, the kings were not causing the excitement. A ten-foot shark appeared below the pier, prompting the fishermen to pull their bluefish out of the water. As the bluefish dangled over the water, the unwanted visitor calmly swam beneath the pier. The shark peered up at the suspended bluefish and waited.

The king fishermen were patiently waiting for the shark to leave. Patience is something the "guys at the end of the pier" must have. For example, Bogue Inlet Pier was having a good year in 2007, with a total of seventy-nine kings. But divide that number of fish among twenty anglers per day in a season that is 160 days long, and you see there was only one king caught on average every other day. That is a whole lot of downtime for a lot of fishermen.

Of course, king fishermen are often rewarded with an acceptable bycatch. Chopper blues, big red drum, amberjacks and tarpon often make a king fisherman's day. One such angler was sixteen-year-old Jesse Lockowitz, who floated out a live bluefish on a balloon rig on September 7, 2005. Lockowitz's reel was rigged with only twenty-pound test as the balloon rig and fish floated about 150 yards out.

A large tarpon took the bait. Lockowitz battled the fish for an hour and half, with the fish leaping out of the water four times. Finally, he got the monster fish near the pier, where it took three gaffs and six people pulling to get the fish to the deck. When it was all over, it was a new state record. The tarpon weighed 175 pounds, was eighty-three inches long and had a forty-two-inch girth. The fish was given to the Division of Marine Fisheries for study.

The Bogue Inlet Pier has other remarkable catches to its credit, including a king mackerel at fifty-eight pounds, several large cobia and a three-hundred-pound tiger shark. On November 9, 2009, Randy McIntyre of Gibsonville, North Carolina, and Bob Funderburk of Maysville, North Carolina, caught dual black drum weighing in at seventy-two pounds, eleven ounces and fifty-eight pounds, five ounces, respectively.

Like every other pier, the Bogue Inlet Pier has suffered through storm damage. In 1955, Hurricane Diane took off 238 feet, and 1996's Fran claimed 400 feet. Hurricane Floyd did some damage as well. But Stanley steadfastly rebuilt the pier to 1,000 feet in length.

Having survived more than forty-five years of bad weather, the biggest threat to the Bogue Inlet Pier came in 2006, when Stanley was looking to sell the property.

Even though he was planning on selling the pier, Stanley was working with the Town of Emerald Isle and developers to ensure that the Bogue Inlet Pier would remain open to the public. The town started an online petition that quickly generated its goal of ten thousand signatures in favor of saving the landmark.

As negotiations dragged on through the summer and into the fall, the town, the developer and Stanley tried to work out an equitable agreement for all. But Emerald Isle's attempt to purchase just the pier and enough parking to make it worthwhile was dead by November 2006. A short time later, the developer pulled out, too, and Mike Stanley took his pier off the market.

The experience left its impression on Emerald Isle mayor Art Schools. In his role as a member of the first North Carolina Waterfront Access Study Committee, Schools made the following comment at a January 9, 2007 meeting: "It's become my opinion that in five to ten years there will be no private piers.

They're all going to be publicly owned if they're there at all. The economics just don't add up for a guy to run a fishing pier anymore without a large subsidy."

Mayor Schools's pronouncement came at the height of a coastal real estate boom. However, after the great economic crash of 2008, sales of waterfront property up and down the coast cooled off faster than a chili dog in a mullet blow. And as this report goes to press, the Bogue Inlet Pier and campground remain. Anglers may well be catching fish there as you are reading this.

HATTERAS ISLAND FISHING PIER/RODANTHE PIER (1960–   )

Hatteras Island has long been known for its outstanding surf, fishing, wild and unpredictable weather and, since 1953, the Cape Hatteras National Seashore. In the early 1930s, Frank Stick—who made his fortune painting cover art for famous New York magazines—had the idea of preserving all the barren lands from the Virginia line to Cape Lookout and keeping them open to the public for recreation and wildlife conservation.

The idea was well received, but as time wore on, the northern beaches around Nags Head became developed. By the time Frank's son, David, became the champion of his father's idea, plans for the Cape Hatteras National Seashore Park were reduced to the stretch of islands from Hatteras to Ocracoke. On January 17, 1953, that land became the Cape Hatteras National Seashore—the nation's first national seashore park. The two million or more people who enjoy visiting Hatteras and Ocracoke Islands every year are indebted to Frank and David Stick.

Until the Herbert C. Bonner Bridge was built in 1963, the only access to Hatteras Island was by ferry. Probably because of this inaccessibility, it was the last of the major inhabited barrier islands to get a fishing pier, in 1960. Until Highway 12 was finished in 1952, Hatteras Island had no paved roads. Still, the island attracted sportsmen because the fishing was outstanding. Just off shore of Hatteras Island, the Gulf Stream is at its closest to the barrier islands. Off Cape Hatteras, the stream combines with the Labrador currents to provide a smorgasbord of fishing opportunities.

In 1960, the Chicamacomico Resort and Motor Lodge built a pier at its location in Rodanthe. The name of the resort and the pier would later be changed to the Hatteras Island Resort and Fishing Pier, and after 2003, when Hurricane Isabel took out the cottages and motel and left only the pier, it became known as the Rodanthe Pier.

Above: Cars had to be ferried over from Oregon Inlet prior to the Herbert C. Bonner Bridge being built in 1963. *Courtesy of the North Carolina State Archives.*

Left: Elvin Hooper with his world record red drum caught in 1973. The record would stand for exactly ten years. *Courtesy of the Outer Banks History Center, Aycock Brown, photographer.*

The Golden Era of Pier Construction

The Rodanthe Pier has been known for large blues, kings and big Spanish mackerel, but it is most famous for red drum. In 1984, during a three-day run, over 140 large red drum were decked. However, the most famous catch was on November 7, 1973, when Elvin Hooper caught a world record red drum of 92.5 pounds.

Fishing all night in the summer was normal for a lot of North Carolina anglers. Most piers were open and staffed all night. Paul Kelmer of Brandon, Florida, remembers one memorable all-night fishing experience from the 1970s at the Rodanthe Pier:

One evening, I decided to spend the entire night on the pier; they were open twenty-four hours back then. I was all set up at the end of the pier with several lines out and waiting for a fish to come along. And I was all alone out there but no big deal. About 1:00 a.m., a group of about five bikers showed up prepared to do some shark fishing.

I watched as they took a fish head about the size of a cantaloupe and put it on a huge hook attached to a six-foot pole with a large conventional reel. They blew up a good-size balloon and tied it to the line about six feet from the fish head. As the wind was blowing offshore, they had no problem putting out about three hundred yards of line. Then everyone except me lay down on the pier and took a snooze. About forty-five minutes later, the reel started to scream and one of the bikers, who looked to be about 250 pounds, jumped up and grabbed the pole. It took him about thirty minutes to bring a ten-foot shark to the pier, but what to do with it? He fought the shark down the side of the pier to the beach. In the meantime, three of the others took off. Two ran down to the edge of the surf, and the third got the pickup and drove it onto the beach so they would have some light.

The guy on the pier finally tossed the rod down to the beach. While the fight continued, the two at the edge of the surf prepared to do their part. The one now fighting the shark brought it in so that as a wave receded, the shark was no longer swimming but stuck on the sand. As the two reached down to grab the shark's tail and drag it up the beach, another wave came in, and suddenly, the shark was swimming and turned toward them. In an instant, the two were literally running on top of the water to get away from the shark. Somewhere in the process, the line broke and the shark swam away. We all spent the next five minutes laughing at the two who had "walked on water." Although I didn't catch any fish that night, I surely enjoyed the entertainment.

Chris Boyles used to fish the Rodanthe Pier in the mid-1980s and also made some remarkable catches. He recalls his first "slammer" bluefish, caught in 1984. It was seventeen pounds, five ounces. Once, when the pier was being rebuilt, a piling started to drift off. Boyles caught it with his snag rig that had thirty-pound test and retrieved it for the pier. The pier owners gave him a six pack for the piling that they told him was worth about $1,500.

Boyles's most remarkable catch came during a nor'easter in November, when he caught a one-pound, ten-ounce Maine lobster. People started to show up at the pier to see the unusual catch, including the game warden, who told Boyles "he needed to confiscate the lobster to conduct a test." When Boyles inquired about what kind of test, the game warden smiled and said, "A taste test." Boyles made the taste test himself and reported that it was a good one.

Rodanthe Pier was once over 1,100 feet long, and it has been shaped and reshaped by the various storms it has endured. In 1999, the combination of Dennis, Floyd, Gert and Irene had a cumulative effect on the pier that took out several of its sections. But the Rodanthe Pier was saved and reopened by June of the next year.

Nor'easters have also claimed several feet of the pier. In March 1989, a spring storm stayed off the coast of the Outer Banks for four days. It washed a half-dozen cottages into the ocean, undercut the Avalon Pier and claimed seventy-five feet of the Rodanthe Pier.

In 2003, the pier outlasted Hurricane Isabel, but the rest of the resort wasn't so lucky, reported pier manager T.J. Cary. The motel, cottages, pool and restaurant were all destroyed. The pier and pier house, however, remained intact, which is more than could be said for the other piers on the Outer Banks.

In a gesture of neighborliness, while they were being repaired the Rodanthe Pier honored the other piers' fishing passes. Said T.J. Cary, "This was one of the most damaging storms to fishing piers in Outer Banks history. Rodanthe Pier has been damaged several times in the past and our fellow piers have been kind enough to extend the same courtesy to us while we rebuilt. Now is our time to repay the kindness."

The pier was 780 feet in 2006, when a Thanksgiving Day storm took off almost 200 feet. The pier was capped and fishing continued, and that is how it remains today.

The buildings from the resort and nearby houses were condemned, and no rebuilding is permitted due to frequent flooding. The sea continues to encroach on the pier and the parking lot is now under sand, as the dune has been pushed back. Yet fishing goes on.

There is no doubt that when the pier was longer it was a beast for landing big fish. A typical year might produce one hundred king mackerel, some in the fifty-pound range. One day in July 1995, anglers decked nine kings and a tarpon. A week before, a fisherman claimed a fifty-two-pound king. By the middle of September 2009, the shorter pier barely had a handful of kings to its credit.

The year 1986 saw Becky East of Midlothian, Virginia, catch a 19-pound bluefish. In 1999, Steve Piece caught a 72-pound, 12-ounce cobia, and in 2002 local Russell Warren landed a 120-pound tarpon.

The Rodanthe Pier was put up for sale in 2006 for $1,225,000 but had no takers. The land on which the pier is located belongs to the National Park Service, and the pier is operated as a concession. The Rodanthe Pier is managed by Marshall Management Company, which also manages hotels and resorts.

The Rodanthe Pier was in the Richard Gere movie *Nights in Rodanthe*. The movie was based on the novel by Nicholas Sparks, and parts of it were filmed on Hatteras Island and on the pier. The house (Serendipity) that was in the movie had to be rescued from the encroaching sea and now sits about a mile farther south in Rodanthe.

MOREHEAD OCEAN PIER (1960–   )

An 80-foot "T" at the end of a pier would be amazing, but imagine it at the end of a pier extending out 1,200 feet into the Atlantic Ocean and you'd have an angler's paradise. From 1960 to 1979 the Morehead Ocean Pier had both of these features. The pier was built right before Hurricane Donna, was destroyed by her and was then immediately rebuilt. In 1979, Hurricane David damaged it again, resulting in the Morehead Ocean Pier being shortened to 800 feet in length.

The Morehead Ocean Pier was purchased by Sheraton Hotels, which built a hotel and rebuilt the pier, though much shorter and without the "T." Hurricane Ophelia in 2005 took out another three hundred feet of the pier. Despite this loss in length, the "Sheraton Pier," as it is now known, is still a wonderful fishing spot.

Tensions between surfers and pier anglers often escalate, as both groups covet the same water. Morehead Ocean Pier was the site of two tragic incidents involving surfers.

In 1964, Larry Capune began making history by logging miles paddling his surfboard. Capune went incredible distances from 1964 to 1987, and the long-distance paddleboarder had racked up an incredible 16,063 miles, including Chicago to Washington via the Great Lakes, St. Lawrence River, the Atlantic Ocean, the Chesapeake Bay and finally the Potomac River.

In 1968, the surfer found himself on his eighteen-foot board at Atlantic Beach. While attempting to go between the pilings at the Morehead Ocean Pier, he was struck in the head by a Coke bottle thrown by the pier's owner, John S. Robbins. Robbins claimed the surfer was "scaring away the fish" and "dropped" three bottles into the water in an effort to scare Capune way.

The third bottle hit its mark, temporarily knocking Capune unconscious. An unidentified person jumped into the water and helped the surfer to shore. Capune needed twenty stitches before he could continue his journey. The case ended up going to court, and the court ruled that a "pier owner does not control the right of under or adjacent to the pier." Taking the law into your own hands is never a good idea.

Another tragic occurrence happened in 1983, when a fisherman died of a heart attack after getting into an argument with two surfers who were in the water on his side of the pier. When the surfers came onto the pier, the man collapsed. No charges were filed in this case. Incidents like these caused communities to enact reasonable barriers around the piers—sometimes marked by floats or flags on the beach—to prevent tempers from flaring.

In the Morehead Ocean Pier's heyday, when it was 1,200 feet long and had that 80-foot T, the fishing was very good. In 1974, eighty-four kings were landed over a weekend, a number of them taken on plugs. A sixty-one-pound black drum, a ninety-four-pound tarpon and a sixty-eight-pound cobia have also been decked on its planks.

IRON STEAMER PIER (1960–2005)

On the morning of June 9, 1864, Captain Burroughs of the Confederate blockade runner *S.S. Pevensey* was looking for the safe port of Wilmington and the protection of the guns at Fort Fisher. The *Pevensey* was built in early 1864 by Stringer, Pembroke and Co. and was to be turned over to the Confederacy once the cost of the ship was paid for by the profits of its voyages. The ship had made three prior successful voyages, but this one was running into trouble.

The crew had miscalculated the course, and the ship was much farther north of Wilmington then they thought. Additionally, in the early morning hours, the vessel was spotted by a Union ship, which proceeded to follow it. The single-stack paddle-wheel steamer had already taken a cannon shot to its deck when it ran aground on Bogue Banks. Before the Union could dispatch boats and capture the ship, a loud explosion occurred on the boat. The *Pevensey* was scuttled by its own crew a few yards from shore.

Ninety-six years later, the Iron Steamer Pier was built next to the *Pevensey* wreck, in what became the town of Pine Knoll Shores. Shelby Freeman bought the oceanfront property on which he built the pier and a motel of the same name in 1959 for only $30,000. The pier was over 1,200 feet long when it was built and had an extension out over the famous shipwreck. That gave the pier an "L" appearance that was very popular with fishermen and sightseers.

Advertisements lauded it as the "longest pier in the state" at over 1,400 feet, including the extension. Advertisements would also show a drawing of the famous paddle-wheeler. The wreck generated a lot of excitement, and anglers generally felt it gave the pier an advantage.

"Freeman owned the pier until 1970 or 1971," according to Newport, North Carolina angler Joel Wolf, a frequent visitor to the Iron Steamer. In addition to being a pier owner, Freeman was an officer and director of the North Carolina Saltwater Sports Fishing Association.

Wolf also recalls that the pier was managed by Lee Schlingman in the 1960s. In the 1970s, it was managed by Jones Cook. Wolf started going to Atlantic Beach on family vacations in 1961, when he was only nine years old. His father, who was in the marines, would often talk about the wonders of the North Carolina coast.

On their first trip to the coastline, Wolf and his family went to the Triple S Pier because Wolf's father was friends with Barry West, who managed the pier at the time. But West had moved on to the Iron Steamer Pier, so the family headed down the road to Pine Knoll Shores. Wolf says the biggest fish he ever saw was the eighty-three-pound tarpon hanging in the pier house at the Iron Steamer Pier.

When he was thirteen, Wolf saw another monstrous fish. "My best recollection is of the cobia caught by Jake Webb Sr. He was using a Mitchell surf reel and twenty-pound test. He fought the fish for over three hours, beached it and then I went with him to Morehead to weigh it. It weighed sixty-eight pounds."

Other large fish were caught on the Iron Steamer Pier as well, even though in the mid-1980s king fishing was prohibited. Several kings in the fifty- to seventy-five-pound range were decked before the ban. A state record Spanish mackerel, weighing eleven pounds, four ounces, was landed in 1971. In later years, some large black drum were caught, one weighing in at eighty-three pounds.

Kris Prichett started fishing the Iron Steamer Pier in 1975 and recalls:

> *I would always tell my dad once we set up our poles, "I'm gonna go fish the wreck," and he would fuss and say, "Every damn time you fish that foolish spot you end up costing me more money than it's worth to bring you." He was referring to the fact that I would lose endless amounts of rigs on the hull of the ship, as I loved fishing right in the center of it at low tide. My dad preferred to fish down toward the end of the pier and never understood why I wanted to fish off the extension. For me, I had visions of the big octopus or some monster fish living inside of the shipwreck, and I had huge plans of landing him and being the talk of the pier.*

The state record sea mullet (three pounds, eight ounces) was caught at the Iron Steamer Pier in 1971 by Ted Drinnon.

Diane N. Funk of Wheaton, Maryland, caught a three-pound, four-ounce sea mullet in 1972 that would have tied the state record had Ten Drinnon not established a new one of three pounds, eight ounces a year before at the Iron Steamer Pier. *Courtesy of the Outer Banks History Center, Aycock Brown, photographer.*

Hanging 1,400 feet out over the ocean would make the pier seem like an easy target for storms, an assumption that proved to be true. After one storm tore out a chunk of the pier, an employee told a newspaper reporter, "The pier takes a beating every time a hurricane passes through the area." Her observation was accurate.

In 1998, Hurricane Bonnie took out the Iron Steamer Pier's famous "L." By the turn of the century, damage from storms forced the owner, Sam McConkey, into bankruptcy, and he basically abandoned the pier after the 2001 fishing season.

Gerald Barfield, a Kinston, North Carolina businessman, purchased the Iron Steamer Pier in 2002. He made repairs and reopened the pier in 2003. By late 2004, Barfield realized his investment wasn't paying off, and in December, he made the difficult decision to close the pier. "It was the hardest decision I've ever made," he told *News and Observer* correspondent Richard Ehrenkaufer as the pier and motel were being torn down and divided into ten individual lots. In the article, Ehrenkaufer wrote prophetically, "Who will be next? Only the accountant's ledger sheet and Mother Nature can tell. And then there were none…?"

There is no disputing the validity of Ehrenkaufer's words. Pier owners get into the business for the love of it, but at some point business decisions need to be made. Too many rebuilds after storms can bankrupt an owner. If a pier is sold, the likelihood of that pier remaining intact is doubtful. Rising real estate values make the return on investment extremely poor, and—especially during a coastal real estate boom—the land is worth more in pieces than it is for a pier business.

New River Inlet Pier (1960–1995)

First known as McKee's Pier, it was built in 1960 and was owned by Bill McKee, who also owned McKee's Ice Company in Wilmington and was once a partner in Barnacle Bill's Pier in Surf City. The pier opened two weeks before the arrival of Hurricane Donna, which destroyed the new attraction. McKee's Pier was rebuilt and extended to over one thousand feet over the Atlantic from its north Topsail Island vantage point.

McKee's Pier was only three miles from the New River Inlet and was built over a rocky bottom. An angler remembering the pier said it was located "at the end of the world" because it was so far from everything else. Another angler recalled that it had a very steep ramp from the ground to the pier house. Advertisements for the pier claimed it was "Where Fisherman Go" and gave the location as "North End of Topsail Island."

Remote or not, being so close to the inlet made McKee's Pier an excellent fishing location. The pier once decked an eighty-six-pound tarpon, as well as several large black and red drum. Even today, with the pier long gone, many Topsail Island trout fishermen have a favorite spot near there. On November 5, 1970, Mrs. Joe Edwards of Garland, North Carolina, tied the thirty-nine-year-old state record for whiting with a three-pound, four-ounce roundhead catch. The record was broken a year later.

In the early 1980s, McKee sold the pier to developer Marlow Bostic, who changed the name to New River Inlet Pier. Bostic was born in 1920 and went from making fifty cents a day working on his family farm in Magnolia, North Carolina, to building multimillion-dollar condos on Topsail Island, north of Surf City.

By the time he became owner of the pier, he was embattled in lawsuits with environmental agencies of the state. Preston Pate, a field services chief for the North Carolina office of Coastal Management, called Bostic "probably the most frequent violator" of state regulations governing shoreline development.

Bostic returned the love, calling the state's Coastal Area Management Act (CAMA) "a waste of money" and saying the enforcement dollars could have been used to purchase the wetlands they were trying to protect. By February 1986, Bostic had racked up over $84,000 in fines from the state.

Marlow Bostic was being battered in the courts, and New River Inlet Pier wasn't faring any better. The pier was closed in 1985 after Hurricane Gloria tore out a large section of the middle. New River Inlet Pier stood vacant at the end of the island until 1990. The pier was never reopened, and eventually it was destroyed by a fire.

In 1994, a federal judge found Marlow Bostic in contempt of court and sentenced him to twenty-one months in jail for refusing to comply with an order to reveal his assets. The sentence was related to lawsuits involving Bostic's real estate activities, not his CAMA violations.

By that time, the northern reaches of Topsail Island were no longer so remote, and the town of North Topsail Beach had been incorporated in 1990. Marlow Bostic's son, Marty Bostic, would serve as its mayor for twelve years.

HOLDEN BEACH PIER (1960–   )

In 1756, Benjamin Holden was granted a purchase patent allowing him to buy land for a plantation and one hundred acres of oceanfront between Lockwood's Folly Inlet and Bacon's Inlet. At that time, when it was low tide, people would walk across the marsh from the mainland to the coast to fish, as well as gather clams and oysters.

In 1926, John Holden built the Holden Beach Resort. The resort was a ten-room guesthouse that had a porch and a stairway to the outhouse in the back. The resort rented rooms for fifteen to twenty dollars a week. In 1932, the Atlantic Intracoastal Waterway (ICW) was dredged, and Holden Beach became a full-time barrier island.

In 1954, Holden Beach was home to three hundred cottages when Hurricane Hazel roared through the island, leaving only five houses intact. It took over ten years before the island would again have three hundred houses.

Holden Beach Fishing Pier was built in 1960 by Lonnie Small, who got a group of investors to help him finance the venture. The pier was built where Meare's or Mary's Inlet once was located. Mary's Inlet was an important location for commercial fishermen in the 1920s and 1930s. The inlet was filled by the tailings when the ICW was dredged in the 1930s. Ironically, Hurricane Hazel opened up another inlet on the same spot in 1954. But it was again filled in, and the pier was built on that spot.

Holden Beach Pier is now owned by Gil Bass, Lonnie Small's son-in-law, and it features a campground, restaurant, gift shop and tackle store. The pier and campground are open all year long. The Holden Beach Pier was the polling location for the town's first election of a mayor after it was incorporated in 1969.

The pier also suffered damage when Hurricane Hugo took out about half of it in 1989, but the pier was rebuilt and opened by April of the next year. When Hurricane Floyd damaged the 1,000-foot pier in 1999, it was rebuilt to its current length of 750 feet.

For Lorne Kime of Mount Gilead, North Carolina, fishing the Holden Beach Pier is a tradition that started when his father took him as a kid. Now Kime takes his son to the same pier. Kime recalls:

> *I have fished at the Holden Beach Fishing Pier all my life. It was a tradition with my father and I to go fishing at the pier every Halloween and Thanksgiving. I remember one Thanksgiving in particular, I believe it was*

Holden Beach Pier featured a wide T until it was taken out by storms in the 1990s. *Courtesy of Holden Beach Pier, Jen-Mar Photo, Charles J. Rogers, photographer.*

1977, when I was fifteen years old. The wind was howling fiercely and the temperature was frigid, but the fish were biting like I had never seen before. We fished through the night, fighting off the cold and catching fish. Since I was a kid, I tried standing downwind with my father blocking the wind to be a little warmer, but to no real avail. We were so busy catching fish that we didn't realize until later that there were only about five other people out there with us. I remember my father looking down the pier and saying, "Son, these are real fishermen." We ran into a problem when it came time for us to go, as, since I was a child, I could not lift my end of the cooler to carry it back to Old Blue, the name given to my father's blue Dodge pickup. Fortunately, one of the other fishermen saw our plight and helped us carry our cooler out. My father is gone now, but I will never forget those times together. I still fish at the pier and hope to create some special memories there with my son.

Fortunately, the Holden Beach Pier remains open.

Riseley Pier (1960–2005)

Riseley Pier was constructed in 1960 on Onslow Beach at the Marine Corps Base at Camp Lejeune. The original purpose of the pier was as an observation platform from which to view landings on the beach. The 1,100-foot pier was complete with bleachers to allow visitors and VIPs an ideal vantage point and relative comfort.

Riseley Pier was named after Brigadier General James Riseley, who graduated from the U.S. Naval Academy in 1922 and was the base's commandant. As a colonel in World War II, Riseley commanded the Marine Corp Sixth Regiment on Okinawa, where he earned the Bronze Star and Legion of Merit.

The pier was dedicated in May 1960 and was almost immediately in danger. A month after the dedication, an amphibious landing vehicle, or "AmTrac," became lodged between the pilings when its driver thought he could make it through the wooden beams. The vehicle remained lodged for a couple of tide changes, battering a hole in the center of the pier.

Marines hit the beach during a training exercise at Camp Lejeune. Riseley Pier originally was built to observe these landings; later it was converted to a fishing pier for camp personnel. *Courtesy of New Hanover Public Library,* Star-News *Archives.*

One local legend has the AmTrac operator as the movie star Steve McQueen, who was stationed at the camp during his stint in the marines. McQueen was known for his outrageous antics at the base, and this story certainly fits with his reputation. As great of a story as this is, it is false. McQueen served in the marines from 1955 to 1957, and by 1960, when the pier was finished, he had already appeared in westerns and had just filmed *The Magnificent Seven*.

Later in 1960, another Landing Craft Utility (LCU) took a chunk out of the Riseley Pier, but the most devastating blow came later that year. On September 12, Hurricane Donna made its third U.S. landfall just south of the pier and pushed northwest, destroying all but one hundred feet of the new pier.

In 1984, the pier was rebuilt to about six hundred feet and converted to a fishing pier for enlisted men. The pier house had a noncommissioned officers' (NCO) quarters on it with rooms that could be reserved a week at a time by servicemen.

In 2003, Hurricane Isabel cut the pier in half. The 321-foot-long remains were still open for fishing in 2005, when Joe Howell from Swansboro, North Carolina, came for a visit. Howell remembered his day fishing in what would be the last days of the Camp Lejeune pier. "I landed a big bluefish there, a dogfish and a seven-pound Spanish mackerel using a live bait on a king rig."

In the fall of 2005, Hurricane Ophelia caused the pier to be closed for good. The rocky bottom on which the pier is built makes it difficult and more expensive to sink pilings and make repairs. In 2006, the camp got $160 million in construction projects designed to improve the life of servicemen at the base. While this seems like a lot of money, it was not enough to repair the pier.

So today the pier stands as Ophelia left it. The fishing gear has been removed, and there are signs that read "WARNING," "Keep Out" and "Risely Pier Closed," with the name of the pier being misspelled. There is a metal gate that keeps people from walking out on the damaged pier, and some of the remaining signs and artifacts from Riseley Pier adorn the NCO club at the base.

Chris Foley, the last pier manager of Riseley Pier, is still hopeful. "We are trying to get the funds from somewhere," he says, smiling. "The marines and their families really enjoyed it."

Scott Hobbs, a U.S. Armed Services veteran, concurs: "I would love for it to get fixed, it sure would be nice for the military guys and gals and their families to have a pier locally."

Chapter 4
The Later Years
1961–1996

E ven after Hurricane Donna did its damage in 1960, North Carolina had twenty-seven commercial fishing piers open for business at the start of 1961. Every major barrier island, with the exception of Sunset Beach, had at least one, including Hatteras Island, which could still only be reached by ferryboat. Piers were now being seen as big business, and they had become a regular part of any tourist or fisherman's trip to the beach.

Piers would continue to be added to the coast for another two decades, but not with the same frequency as in the 1950s. The last new pier to be built on the North Carolina coast would be the Seaview on Topsail Island, which opened in 1984. For the next twelve years, the number of piers available to fishermen would number right around thirty-five.

The thirty-five years from 1961 to 1996 were a period when the pier business truly thrived. In the '80s and '90s, the numbers of fish caught, especially red drum, were declining, but piers remained a good, inexpensive way to fill up a cooler with fish. These years were also relatively free from damaging storms and hurricanes. There would be the Ash Wednesday Storm of 1962, Hurricane Hugo in 1989 and the "Storm of the Century" in 1993, but for the most part it was an extended period of quiet hurricane seasons. In this period, the weather was a minor nuisance compared to storms of the previous ten years.

An amazing thing about the "Hurricane Alley" years of the '50s is that every pier that was damaged or destroyed was rebuilt, with the exception of Fort Fisher Pier and an unnamed pier under construction at Carolina Beach that was destroyed by Hazel.

One reason these piers were repaired after storms is that construction costs were still relatively low. Materials, such as pine pilings, could be obtained from North Carolina's vast forests. Also, land for the building of oceanfront cottages and condos was not yet in high demand, which left a lot of space open for the development of piers.

Vacations continued to grow in popularity, so traveling families needed more activities at the beach. Bowling alleys, roller-skating rinks, miniature golf courses and movie houses appeared, but piers continued to be a popular diversion. The beach communities that had, in many cases, grown up around a pier continued to grow. The pier culture, and the culture of the state's small beach towns, changed surprisingly little for over three decades.

Then the Atlantic began spawning powerful hurricanes once again. Five made landfall in North Carolina in the three years from 1996 to 1999. This new round of storms, combined with an unprecedented building boom that saw the price of waterfront lots reach $1 million and more, would eventually threaten the very survival of pier fishing on our coast.

DOLPHIN PIER (1961–1983)

In 1961, the Dolphin Pier was built in Topsail Beach, splitting the distance between the Surf City and the Jolly Roger and giving the twenty-two-mile island its sixth ocean pier. The Dolphin Pier was part of an entire complex designed to maximize vacationers' time at the beach. Across the street from the pier, the complex had a marina featuring a boat ramp, boat rentals, boat storage and even a head boat for charter called *Buddy's Pirate*.

The beach side of the complex had the Dolphin Pier plus a life-guarded beach, complete with picnic tables and umbrellas. The pier had a grill, arcade and twenty-four-hour tackle shop that featured live bait.

The Dolphin Pier complex was built by Harvey Jones, who might have had the first residence on the island when he floated a house from the mainland across the Intracoastal Waterway. In the 1970s, the pier was owned by Frank Bowman, who also owned two small grocery stores on Topsail.

Like many of the businesses on the coast, the Dolphin Pier understood that it was providing a unique opportunity to a somewhat captive audience and tried to appeal to tourists as well as die-hard sportsmen. Heather Pierce Smith's grandparents owned the Topsail Motel from 1974 to 1979, and she recalls the summers there and going to the Dolphin Pier to buy ice cream: "My sister and I would spend a lot of time walking up to the Jolly Roger Pier then back to the Dolphin Pier. The motel was pretty much in the middle of the two piers."

While some would remember the other entertainment values of the pier, anglers recall that the Dolphin Pier produced excellent catches. "They caught a lot of big fish up there," said veteran Jolly Roger fisherman Angelo DePaola. "It was a good trout pier too," he added. Indeed, the Dolphin Pier was known for both; archived fishing reports from the *Wilmington Morning News* read like an honor roll for anglers.

Sid Soos, along with his two sons, Charlie and Keith, caught nine kings in one day on the Dolphin Pier. On another occasion, Charlie caught a 115-pound tarpon.

Larry Burchett, of Virginia, decked an 81-pound tarpon in 1981, and in 1983, E.A. Goode managed to land a 105-pound tarpon. Henry Bettis caught a 48-pound tarpon in 1978. The first tarpon of the 1982 fishing season, a 47-pounder, was caught by Julian Cantrell of Asheville. The first tarpon caught in 1972 at the pier was a 68-pounder, caught by Paul Woody of Fayetteville in the first week of July.

In 1983, Terry McPherson caught a one-hundred-pound tarpon on the Dolphin Pier. It was his third tarpon of the year, and it was not his biggest catch. Later in the year, pier manager Ransom Smith reported that McPherson had caught one hundred Virginia mullet using sand fleas.

In 1979, the *Wilmington Morning Star* reported that Dick Wiley of Manlius, New York, caught a three-pound, twelve-ounce sea mullet. If this was the case, it was never reported to the North Carolina Division of Marine Fisheries, because the current record listed is Drinnon's at three pounds, eight ounces caught from the Iron Steamer Fishing Pier. Another large sea mullet was caught in 1982 by Jean Fincher, who hit the scales with a one-pound, twelve-ounce fish.

On September 22, 1970, Larry Lee established a new state record for Spanish mackerel when he took a ten-pound, six-ounce fish to the scales. Lee was one of the pier's most accomplished fishermen. His name was all over the leader board at the Dolphin Pier, and earlier in the same year, he set a state record with a crevalle jack caught at the Surf City Pier.

Earl Wooten of Gastonia, North Carolina, caught a sixty-eight-pound cobia on the Dolphin Pier in June 1980 and then followed it up in August of that year by filling two coolers with pompano and whiting caught on sand fleas.

In one week in 1980, fishermen on the Dolphin Pier caught thirty-one kings. In 1981, the biggest king was a thirty-five-pound, four-ounce fish caught by Bob Peterson of Chapel Hill. Earlier that year, Beth Howard won

Pier owners would promote the large and spectacular catches on their piers as a way to attract visitors to their pier. *Courtesy of the Outer Banks History Center, Aycock Brown, photographer.*

the Topsail Island King Mackerel Tournament that was sponsored by the Topsail Island Fishing Club with a twenty-six-pound, ten-ounce fish.

The Dolphin Pier also had a reputation of being a great location from which to catch speckled trout. Shorty Mills of Charlotte caught 162 pounds of the fish there in November 1980. A few weeks earlier, Charlie Fencher and two friends from Jacksonville, Florida, went home with 132 pounds of speckled trout. Later, Charlie returned with his wife and caught another sixty-five trout.

In 1980, Frank Bowman sold the pier and surrounding property to the Island Development Corporation. Although it wasn't clear at the time, the Dolphin's days were numbered.

The Island Development Corporation planned to build condominiums on the sound side of the property and call the complex Queen's Grant. They selected this name because the land that the pier was on was once part of a grant from the Queen of England—or so the legend went.

While the condos were being built, the pier continued to produce fish. Danny Rambeaux first managed it for the new owners, and then Ransom Smith took over. After the 1983 fishing season, the pier closed for renovations. Unfortunately for anglers, the pier remained closed. In 1987, there was hope that the Dolphin Pier might once again be repaired and reopened, but issues in getting a sewer line installed held up plans for a second grand opening.

The following year, there was again talk of the Dolphin Pier being reopened, but this time as a private pier for the owners and guests of Queen's

Grant. Again, this did not happen. After a while, reopening was no longer even discussed. The pilings were cut off at the surface of the ocean. The decision to do this was kind of a head scratcher for some. "It seems to me it would be dangerous to boaters," says Doug Medlin.

Even when it was nothing but submerged pilings, the Dolphin Pier continued to be popular with trout fishermen. A group even went to the Topsail Beach commissioners and asked them for better access and additional parking. Years after the pier was gone, "where the Dolphin Pier was" continued to appear on fishing reports. Today it is not evident that there was ever a pier there. If the pilings are still out there they are not visible, even at low tide.

SUNSET BEACH PIER (1961–   )

Mannon Gore purchased the three-mile barrier known as Sunset Beach in 1955 from the Brooks family and International Paper Company. Sunset Beach is the southernmost barrier island in North Carolina. In the late 1950s, a one-lane pontoon swing bridge was built over the Intracoastal Waterway that would allow vehicle traffic to finally reach the little island.

Mannon Gore was the son of a farmer who became the driving force in developing both Sunset Beach and Ocean Isle Beach. The famous pontoon bridge was also one of Gore's designs. In 1963, the town of Sunset Beach became incorporated.

The original structure, first called Vesta Pier, was built out to 1,100 feet in 1961. The name came from a Confederate blockade runner that ran aground in February 1864. When the Confederate captain could not sneak into the mouth of the Cape Fear River with the *Vesta*, he tried to go past the blockade and head to Georgetown, South Carolina, but was spotted. Instead of letting the ship fall into Union hands, Confederates set it on fire, and the remains of the ship sunk off the beach. The same day the *Vesta* went down another blockade runner, the *Ranger*, went down a few miles north at Holden Beach.

Even before the pier was built on Sunset Beach, fishermen would swim out to the *Vesta* wreck at low tide, stand on the boiler and fish for sheepshead and drum. Later, after the pier had been built, divers reported that the hull of the twin steamer was in good condition and that the ship was sitting parallel to the shore. The cargo holds of the vessel were all intact, and only a few of the ship's fittings had been removed. You could tell where the ship was buried, as there was a longer gap between the pilings. By 1970, the ship was completely buried by sand.

For years the pier has been called both the Vesta Pier and the Sunset Beach Pier, but the latter name seems to be more popular.

Sunset Beach has some of the whitest sand on the coast and the pier extends a couple hundred feet out over the sand before it spans water, which makes it an ideal location for beachgoers to find shade from the hot sun. From the deck of the pier, the high-rise hotels in North Myrtle Beach are visible.

The long, shallow beach is not ideal for surf fishing, but the location of the pier helps. The Sunset Beach Pier extends out to deeper water, and because it is so close to inlets on either side, the pier is productive. Although the pier has decked its share of kings, it is more commonly known for those species that favor sandy bottoms—flounder, sea mullet, trout and pompano.

You can find many things on a pier, including romance. Brooke and David Bowman from West End, North Carolina, go pier fishing a lot, and Sunset Beach is their favorite place. They first went there over ten years ago. "We carved our initials on the pier when we were dating," Brooke Bowman recalls. "We can still see our initials." The Bowmans now take their daughter there to see them as well.

The current pier has a restaurant, gift shop and tackle store. While there is a charge for parking, it is deducted from the price of the pier permit. Because there is a shortage of parking on Sunset Beach, beachgoers gladly give up the five-dollar fee.

A new bridge is now open, replacing the pontoon bridge and alleviating the traffic problems that used to plague weekend visitors. There is talk about converting the pontoon bridge to a fishing pier in the Intracoastal Waterway. Currently, that location is an excellent spot for red drum and trout.

FRISCO PIER (1962–2008)

During Easter weekend of 2009, an angler bought bait at Frank and Fran's Tackle shop in Avon. As the fisherman peered at the fishing report board, he read about puppy drum, blues, croaker whiting and even pompano. The space allocated for the Frisco Pier report was curiously vacant. "No report from Frisco?" the man asked.

"The pier is not opened," replied the woman behind the counter. "It needs repairs and no one knows when it is going to happen," she continued. "If they start now they could get it opened for the summer, but it may not reopen at all."

As it turns out, the pier—built in 1962—didn't open at all in 2009, and its fate is still up in the air.

The future of Frisco Pier is in doubt. The pier has not placed an angler out of the water since 2008. Here is the pier in the fall of 2010. *Photo by Al Baird.*

Originally known as the Cape Hatteras Fishing Pier, in recent years it came to be called the Frisco Pier. It was never very long—only about 600 feet when it first was built. The Frisco Pier has varied in length over the years, due to various damages and repairs, but for the most part it has stayed between 450 and 600 feet long. Many anglers lament the fate of the popular pier and recall good memories of the place.

Danny Daniels, fifty, from St. Albans, West Virginia, first went to Hatteras Island when he was twelve. He stayed at the KOA campground in Rodanthe and fished the Cape Hatteras Fishing Pier when it held the world record for Hooper's red drum, but Daniels calls Frisco Pier his favorite.

"I have fond memories of the Frisco Pier," says Daniels. "I caught my first big drum there, my first king there and my first cobia there." Daniels recalls his cobia: "I had two rods out at the time and they both had cobia strikes at the same time. I told the guy next to me to grab the other rod, I got mine in but he lost the one he had."

Frisco Pier is the only south-facing pier on the Outer Banks. It sits in the concaved basin protected by Cape Point to the east and Hatteras Inlet to the west. The location of Frisco Pier gives Hatteras Island anglers an option when dealing with the severe nor'easters that frequent the island. While the east-facing piers have to deal with muddy water and high wind, Frisco Pier's water can be clear and calm. Daniels thinks this could be one reason the pier has been so productive for kings and other large predatory fish.

Paul Kelmer, from Brandon, Florida, agrees with Daniels. Kelmer first visited Hatteras Island in 1953, when he was nine. "I have been returning to Hatteras Island for the past fifty-plus years. I have fished Rodanthe, Avon and Frisco Piers, although Frisco is my favorite." Kelmer says his dream is to win the lottery and buy his favorite pier.

Kelmer fished Frisco Pier in the early 1980s and then stopped coming when he moved to Florida. His daughter, however, made a trip back to visit relatives and got a surprise when looking at the picture board at the pier. Kelmer says:

In the early '80s, I migrated my vacations southward on Hatteras Island and began fishing at the Frisco Pier. August was not the greatest time for pier fishing, especially for king mackerel, cobia and red drum, and those fish were my targets of choice. During one week, I managed to catch a nineteen-pound king and a twenty-three-pound channel bass. Of course, I went through the weighing and picture taking at the pier house. After returning home to upstate New York, I had the film developed, found the best shots of me and my fish, labeled them and mailed them back to the Frisco Pier. Unfortunately, I didn't get back to Hatteras for a number of years.

In the meantime, my brother, his wife and their three sons moved to Hatteras Village. In 1983, we had moved to Tampa, Florida, and I was enjoying saltwater fishing close to my new home. In 1989, when my daughter was sixteen, she said that she would like to visit her cousins at Hatteras. She was given a "locals" tour of Hatteras Island, along with the normal teenage gossiping. One of their stops was at Frisco Pier, which I had never stopped talking about. After a couple of minutes of her checking out the pictures on the bulletin board, a cry was heard: "That's my dad!" Sure enough, there were the two pictures I had mailed to the pier seven or eight years earlier. My daughter finally learned that I hadn't been telling fish stories about the ones I caught at the Frisco Pier. I still go back to Hatteras when I can, but it never seems to be often enough.

David Bowman recalls fishing on the Frisco Pier with his good friend Andy Carpenter in 2005:

The Later Years

I had not seen Andy in a long, long time since he was undergoing surgery for cancer and had a long recovery time, so this was a special trip in getting to see a friend after a long absence.

We had set out early in the morning to surf fish, but the current was so strong that we decided to fish from Cape Hatteras Fishing Pier. We fished all day and caught small blues and sugar trout. Around early evening we decided to call it a day, but Andy wanted to make one more cast on the north side of the pier. A few minutes later, Andy landed his first red drum that was in the eighteen- to twenty-seven-inch slot limit.

Piers offer a unique experience to everyone, even those who do not fish. Sightseers walking the beach often detour out on the planks to view the water, gaze at the beach and participate in the excitement of the pier's anglers. Donald Zawacki of Syracuse, New York, is one of those non-fishermen who remembers the Frisco Pier. "We loved the Frisco Pier, especially at night when it was all lit up. Sometimes our family would have picnics on it and just enjoy the scenery."

Like the other piers on Hatteras, Frisco Pier is known for drum fishing as well as large bluefish. Garry Oliver has said, "Bluefish is what put the Outer Banks on the map as far as fishing goes." Although the island is now more famous for red drum, it was the pictures of baseball bat–length chopper blues seen in newspapers all over the East Coast that first attracted anglers to Hatteras Island. The world record bluefish, caught in 1972 by James Hussey, was pulled out of the water a few miles west of the Frisco Pier at Hatteras Inlet. Hussey's record catch was thirty-one pounds, twelve ounces, and most people believe that it will never be topped.

Frisco Pier has had its share of monster fish but maybe less than its fair share of record-breaking catches. For years Frisco Pier had no phone, so earlier catches went largely unrecorded. But the accounts of anglers and the picture board at the Frisco Pier tell a different story. A seventy-six-pound tarpon and cobias weighing in at sixty-four and seventy-five pounds are on the board. Another angler got an eight-pound false albacore, and a seventy-seven-pound tarpon was decked in 1992.

In 1980, James Beagle of Norfolk, Virginia, caught a twelve-pound, twelve-ounce Spanish mackerel that established a new state record and beat the old record, held by Ralph Drawhorn, by over a pound. Beagle used a live bluefish as bait.

In the late 1990s, Brient Jackson of Frisco began making an angling name for himself at the age of thirteen. Jackson caught a fifty-five-pound cobia to

James Hussey of Tarboro, North Carolina, with his world record bluefish caught a few miles southwest of the Frisco Pier. *Courtesy of the Outer Banks History Center, Aycock Brown, photographer.*

go along with a couple of forty-pounders he had caught the year before. In 1996, he landed a seventy-five-pound tarpon off the Frisco Pier.

Frisco Pier was originally built by several families who lived in or vacationed near Frisco, and the current owners are Tod and Angie Gaskill, who bought the pier after Hurricane Isabel and have made numerous repairs. The land is owned by the National Park Service. Before failing to open in 2009, Gaskill told the *Island Free Press* that he needed $50,000 to $75,000 to make repairs and, considering the economy, he didn't think it would be worth it.

A year later, the estimate grew to $175,000 or $200,000 to reopen Frisco Pier. That estimate could be low, as the pier lost another five pilings in 2009 to Hurricane Bill (a storm that remained offshore). The pier suffered more damage from surf churned up by Hurricane Earl in 2010, and it still remains closed.

AVALON PIER (1962–   )

In 1962, the northern Outer Banks got its fifth pier when the Avalon Pier was built around milepost six on the Virginia Dare Road. Despite damage incurred from storms, the length of the pier has always remained about 650 to 700 feet. The pier is currently owned and operated by Dare Resorts, Inc. At one point it was owned by Walter Davis, who had also famously purchased the Kitty Hawk Pier so that he could enjoy an Orange Crush.

In some years, Cape Hatteras is close to the southern edge of the striped bass winter migration in North Carolina. The years that stripers make an early entrance into North Carolina, Avalon Pier is an ideal location to fish them. The pier typically closes in late November/early December, so the season is short if they do arrive.

The Avalon Pier regularly decks thirty-pound kings, as well as large drum and big bluefish. The use of Got-Cha lures is common, as the man behind the counter noted: "We sell more of the red head and white body lure than all the rest of them combined." The Avalon Pier is also good for speckled trout and flounder.

Striped bass caught on an Outer Banks pier. Avalon Pier's northern position gives it an advantage when the stripers come south. *Courtesy of the Outer Banks History Center, Aycock Brown, photographer.*

In 1990, B.T. Smith, a paper factory worker from New Kent, Virginia, caught a forty-pound sailfish from the end of the pier. The pier has also reeled in a sixty-two-pound amberjack.

As with most northern Outer Banks Piers, for many years the chopper bluefish blitz occurred in the late fall at Avalon Pier. Newspapers reported acres of bluefish attacking baitfish, usually menhaden. But sometimes the prey was speckled trout, with the bigger, hungry blues often driving them up to the beach. Locals claim to have picked up five- to seven-pound trout that had beached themselves to get away from the bluefish.

By the late 1980s, these types of blitzes were becoming less and less frequent. Bluefish were being overfished and, unfortunately, in some cases needlessly slaughtered. Today, when a blitz occurs someone always remarks that it is just like the old days.

In 1989, the Mid-Atlantic Fisheries Management Council recommended a ten-fish daily limit on bluefish. The plan was approved by the Atlantic States Marine Fisheries Commission and went into effect in 1990. The plan seems to have worked. Today, bluefish are listed as viable and have a fifteen-fish daily limit with a five-fish limit on those bigger than twenty-four inches.

The Avalon Pier has a grill, sells bait and tackle and has fishing gear that can be rented. Avalon Pier has the biggest arcade room of any pier in the state and has a shaded porch from which visitors can take in the action on the planks.

AVON FISHING PIER (1964–   )

It was one year after the opening of the Herbert C. Bonner Bridge over Oregon Inlet that Hatteras Island got its third and final pier. The Avon Pier opened in 1964, and almost immediately, pictures of sportsmen posing with large drum started hitting the newspapers in North Carolina and Virginia.

Some of those pictures are still on display on the walls of the pier house.

The Outer Banks may have been put on the fisherman's map by large bluefish, but when you think of Hatteras Island you automatically think of red drum. Big ones. If you are targeting a record-breaking catch, timing and location are two key elements. If you are targeting a record-breaking red drum, then between the Rodanthe Pier and the Avon Pier in early November would be the ideal place and time to catch one.

Jack Scott with his world record red drum caught on the Avon Pier in 1970. The record would stand until Elvin Hooper broke it in 1983. *Courtesy of the Outer Banks History Center, Aycock Brown, photographer.*

Consider the evidence. On November 9, 1970, Jack Scott, from Colonial

Heights, Virginia, caught an eighty-two-pound channel bass from the Avon Pier. Three years later, on November 7, Elvin Hooper made his record-breaking catch at the Rodanthe Pier. Exactly ten years after that, David G. Deuel broke that record with a ninety-four-pound, two-ounce fish caught while surf fishing just north of Avon Pier. Deuel's fish is still a world record.

Aycock Brown. The legendary photographer was known to drop everything and head off with his camera if he got word of a big catch. *Courtesy of the North Carolina State Archives.*

The red drum is the official state fish of North Carolina for many reasons. The importance of the fish cannot be overstated. Sports anglers enjoy the battle with the fish, and red drum are also important to commercial fishers. In the mid-1950s, concern over the depletion of the species from overfishing came to the forefront. Rules were enacted for both groups of anglers that limited the daily catch to only two of the large-breed redfish. The current regulation calls for only one drum allowed to be taken in the eighteen to twenty-seven slot size. Nothing outside this range is permitted.

Avon Pier has been a favorite of fishermen since it was built. The pier, like others on the island, has varied in length due to the pounding of storms but has always provided amenities that tourists and fishermen have needed. There was a thirty-eight-unit campground at the location until the late 1980s.

Bob Langston remembers playing at the pier for a Fourth of July celebration:

Back in 1986, I was living in Manteo. When the year began, I was a starving DJ doing overnight shifts for WOBR, Beach 95 FM in Wanchese. WOBR had an AM station that played country, or beach country. The only regular employee was a guy named Dallas Morris. Dallas wanted to put together a country band. I had a bass, and he needed a bass player.

Dallas booked us to play the Fourth of July party at the Avon Pier. Because of the campground there, they had a bunch of folks around for the Fourth. Early in the day, the pier folks had steamed a bunch of crabs and had a big picnic.

At the time, there was a bathhouse located about where Dirty Dicks is now. We set up on the back porch and played for the beer fest and dance for about four hours that night. Didn't fish, but then there was a day when the piers were really more of an activity center, and not just a place to drown bait.

The pier closed in 1988, and plans for a Days Inn Motel were drawn up. The planned motel never materialized, and the pier did not reopen until 1991. Frank and Fran Folb, of Frank and Fran's Tackle Shop in Avon, became the new operators of the three-hundred-foot pier.

While all of the piers have had to deal with hurricanes, the two facing east on Hatteras Island have had as much damage from nor'easters. Almost immediately after the Avon Pier was refurbished, a spring storm hit and caused the planks to buckle. The Avon Pier now has the distinctive look of an old wooden roller coaster, complete with banked turns. The end of the pier forms a cross, as there is a small end that extends outward from the T.

The Avon Pier has varied in length from almost 1,000 feet in the 1960s to about 300 feet when it reopened in 1991. The current pier extends about 525 feet over water. The current owner is Ed Nunnally, from Virginia, and the current manager is Keith Matthews. The Avon Pier has a gift shop, snack bar and tackle shop. Not only does Avon Pier feature the only miniature golf course of any pier in the state, but the course is natural grass. The Atlantic Cafe is located at the end of the lot.

In early September 2009, Kenny West, from Midlothian, Virginia, got his pink Got-Cha plug in the right location, hooking an Atlantic bonito. The hard-swimming fish worked him from the left corner of the Avon Pier to its center section, which makes the cross. He finally got the fish close enough to the pier for another angler to net his prize.

Bonito are a rare treat for pier anglers, and it is best to take them like Kenny West did, on light tackle with a plug and dozens of witnesses.

Scotch Bonnet Pier (1966–1996)

In 1966, Topsail Island got its eighth pier when the Scotch Bonnet was erected just north of Surf City. Lewis Williamson's one-thousand-foot pier quickly began to make a name for itself.

The Later Years

Reports from Williamson on catches made at Scotch Bonnet Pier regularly ran in the *Wilmington Star News* fishing section, and they are staggering compared to today's reports:

From Scotch Bonnet Pier fishing reports in the newspaper's archives:

- Jerry Rhine of Fayetteville had 135 sea mullets in one outing.
- Willie Parish of Goldsboro caught 200 spots.
- Ken Royals of Jacksonville hauled in 11 flounders in one outing.
- June 1971, Jack Hodges caught five kings in one day.
- Mark Tolletsby caught a 53-pound cobia in July of 1972.
- 23 kings were landed in one day in 1976.
- A 62-pound cobia was decked in 1977.
- In 1980 EA Goode landed an 83-pound tarpon.
- July of 1980, Harvey Kindell of Goldsboro matched Hodges by catching five of his own kings in one day, the largest weighing in at 26 pounds.
- Patrick Powell of Goldsboro landed a 19-pound bluefish in 1980.

Scotch Bonnet Pier featured a campground, tackle shop, gift shop and arcade, as well as a restaurant and lounge. It even had a bathhouse for beachgoers to change in and out of their swimsuits. Scotch Bonnet Pier was a common meeting place for various clubs and groups in the community. Jeff Cavenaugh, from Teachey, North Carolina, grew up going to the pier with his parents and grandparents. Later he would make the trip on his own.

When I got older and got my driver's license I would go to the pier to fish, and just to the area north of the pier was the beach hangout for all my schoolmates as well as myself. We would hang out at the beach and go up to the restaurant for burgers and to play games at the arcade. We would go spot fishing in the fall. My family had a trailer just north of the pier on Wahoo Street until Hurricane Fran took the pier as well as several trailers, campers and cottages.

In the late 1980s, the land where the pier stood was annexed into Surf City. Over the years, the pier suffered from a number of storms, including the "Storm of the Century" nor'easter that caused $100,000 damage in 1993. Bertha and Fran in 1996 caused about $1 million in damage and pretty much finished the pier, which was then part owned by Wylie Page.

All that remains today of the Scotch Bonnet Pier are two pilings connected by a cross beam. There is a public handicapped beach access where the pier once stood.

Ocean Crest Pier (1968–)

In 1968, Ocean Crest Pier became the last pier of the decade to be built in North Carolina and the third and last pier to be built on Oak Island. By the end of the 1960s, pier construction had practically stopped. There was a pier on every major populated barrier island. In high tourist areas there were several, with some located just barely a decent cast away from one another.

The relatively calm weather in the 1960s and 1970s, along with the increase in coastal vacationers, made operating a pier a profitable business. Ocean Crest Pier was poised to take its share of the pier fishing trade and, in the 1970s, ran ads in fishing guides and vacation magazines claiming that its pier "was the newest and longest on the North Carolina Coast."

Warren Calloway built Ocean Crest Pier and added the motel in 1972, both of which he operated with his wife, Maxine. Calloway was a World War II veteran and was stationed in the Philippines with the Railroad Battalion.

Ocean Crest Pier was located between Yaupon Pier to the east and Long Beach Pier to the west, and it quickly proved to be a fisherman's favorite. Vance Jones from Clayton, North Carolina, started going to Ocean Crest Pier and staying at the Ocean Crest Motel right after they were built. "I have spent many days and evenings as a child with my father on our annual trips to Ocean Crest motel and pier," Jones said. "I am thirty-eight now and started fishing the piers with my father at the tender age of one year old. In fact, one of the worst sunburns I ever got was on that pier because I didn't want to go back to the room, thinking as kids do that I would miss some of the excitement and wonderment of what was going to be pulled up next."

Jones was right about wondering what was going to be pulled up next. North Carolina piers offer some of the widest variety of fish species found anywhere, and Ocean Crest Pier has been very productive, even for young anglers. In fact, young anglers seem to have more success there than at any other pier. In May 1984, Teresa Nelson, who was eleven at the time, landed a twenty-four-pound, eight-ounce king on Ocean Crest Pier.

King fishing at Ocean Crest Pier often matched or topped king fishing at the other piers. The same weekend that Long Beach Pier had its incredible run in 1979, Ocean Crest Pier decked thirty kings. Such productivity at Ocean Crest Pier was the norm, not the exception. In 1982, thirty-four kings were gaffed on one June day, and twelve were caught the next day. From October 14 to October 16, 1989, 49 kings were decked on Ocean Crest Pier. In 2007, the pier decked 179 kings and, two years prior, decked over 150.

The Later Years

In June 1989, Bo Crump of Southport, North Carolina, caught a 50.5-pound cobia at Ocean Crest Pier. Crump was no stranger to catching large fish at the pier, and in May 1998 he landed a 53-pound, six-ounce king and a 41-pound, five-ounce smoker king in the same day.

In August 1982, Sammy Broome, twelve, battled and landed a one-hundred-pound tarpon at Ocean Crest Pier. Broome finally beached the huge silver king, only the third tarpon to be caught from this pier, over a mile down the coast using only twenty-pound test line. The day after Broome landed his tarpon, Wayne Tillian of Greensboro, North Carolina, caught the pier's fourth tarpon, a ninety-one-pounder.

Ocean Crest Pier has held a couple of state records for fish over the years. The first record was established by Roy D. Ward of Greensboro when he caught a one-pound, nine-ounce spot in October 1971. (The current record holder for spot is a one-pound, thirteen-ounce fish that was caught at Mann's Harbor in 1979.)

The second record catch happened on September 4, 2009, when Thomas Cutler, of Oak Island, North Carolina, hooked and landed a twenty-seven-pound, seven-ounce tripletail on a strip of flounder belly. The thirty-five-inch fish barely fit into the pier net. Tripletails are named because of their three rounded fins that all resemble a tail. They are typically found from the Chesapeake Bay south to the Gulf of Mexico, and they are a very shy fish that are rarely taken from piers.

Cutler spotted the fish and made several attempts at getting it to bite. Finally, he decided to loosen the drag and place the rod down and back away from the rail so as not to spook the fish. It worked. The fish took the bait, and he had a state record.

Ocean Crest Pier was completely wiped out by Hurricane Floyd in 1999, and parts of the pier were found two miles down the coast. Despite all the damage, Ocean Crest Pier was reopened the next year.

Storms were not its only enemy. On Saturday, January 29, 1995, Ocean Crest Pier was struck by a 65-foot shrimp boat, the *Arcelia*, which took 125 feet off the end of the pier. The operators of the boat were given sobriety tests, which they failed. Wade Goin, who owned the pier at that time with his wife, Ruth, estimated the damage at $150,000.

Today, Ocean Crest Pier is operated by Dave Cooper. Cooper has a loyal following among fishermen and is one of the reasons the pier is so popular. Anthony Wright of Burlington, North Carolina, said, "For many years, my wife and I have enjoyed the hospitality of Dave Cooper and the folks at the Ocean Crest Pier."

Ocean Crest Pier sells everything you will need while over the water. The Island Way restaurant is located right next door, and the Ocean Crest motel is still located on site but is not under the same management as the pier.

INDIAN BEACH FISHING PIER (1974–1998)

Bogue Banks' eighth and final pier was built in 1974 at Indian Beach, which got its name when Earl Thompson, of Thompson Steel Pier fame, found an Indian mound on some nearby property. Indian Beach Fishing Pier was owned by Ken Heverly, who also owned Emerald Isle Pier.

Indian Beach Fishing Pier, which also featured a campground, varied in length from about 800 to 1,200 feet, depending on what storms had just gone through. In 1996, after Hurricane Bertha took out the dune and Fran did substantial damage, Heverly agonized over whether to repair and reopen the pier. Finally he decided to rebuild and reopen it. But in 1998, Hurricane Bonnie damaged the pier, and then Hurricane Floyd destroyed

Indian Beach Pier was the last pier built on Bogue Banks, and it had the shortest lifespan of only twenty-four years. *Courtesy of the Carteret County Historical Society, Inc., Morehead City, North Carolina.*

it the next year. At that point, Heverly threw in the towel and closed the pier for good.

Having survived only twenty-four years, Indian Beach Fishing Pier had one of the shortest life spans of any pier, but it produced its share of big fish, including a state record tarpon caught by John W. Freeman in 1978. Freeman's tarpon was a 164-pound fish, and the record stood until it was broken on the nearby Bogue Inlet Pier by young Jesse Lockowitz's silver king in 2005. Another 108-pound tarpon was caught in 1982, and the pier regularly took in over ten kings daily.

In July 1982, Jim Tucker of Raleigh, North Carolina, caught a 108-pound tarpon on Indian Beach Fishing Pier. Later in the fall of that year, a twelve-foot shark created havoc when it took two king rigs and broke both lines.

A few years earlier, in 1980, a number of shark sightings closed the beaches, but the piers remained opened. There were seventeen reports of a variety of sharks, including hammerheads, tigers, black-tip and spinners. This unusually high number of sharks was blamed on water temperatures, which had reached well past eighty degrees.

Where the pier once stood is public beach (or "CAMA") access point #5 on Salter Path Road at milepost 12. The area is wooded with ten parking spaces.

SEAVIEW PIER (1984–   )

The last pier to be built in the century was Seaview Pier, built about 1984. It was originally called Salty's Pier and was built on North Topsail Beach, with the New River Inlet Pier to the north and Paradise Pier to the south. Seaview Pier was destroyed by the famous "Storm of the Century" in 1993 but was rebuilt and reopened in 1999.

In 2000, the pier was bought by Greg Ludlum, its current owner, who embarked on his "labor of love" by becoming a pier owner. In an interview for the North Carolina Fishing Pier Society (NCFPS) website in 2007, Ludlum was quick to point out the costs of running a pier, and he realizes that the land is worth more without the pier (for oceanfront housing) than with the pier, but he says he is committed to providing the service of the fishing pier to the public. "This is my life," Ludlum said. "What's happening to the piers is killing me."

Ludlum's pier is impressive. It is one of the many on the coast that claim to be 1,000 feet in length, which seems to be a kind of status symbol for

The Seaview Pier in the early 1990s. The motel was added later and is located just south of the pier house. *Courtesy of Missiles and More Museum.*

pier owners. Some claim their piers to be 1,000 feet long regardless of their true length. Seaview Pier has at least 1,000 feet of planks, and according to measurements taken from Google Earth, it has more feet over water (875) than any other pier in the state.

Seaview Pier features a complete tackle store that sells bait and beach supplies, rents tackle and freely gives advice. The second floor of the pier house has a restaurant, which has a variety of menu items and a deck that overlooks the pier. This deck has one of the best views of the Atlantic Ocean that you can find anywhere.

While Seaview Pier is known for bottom fishing, the guys at the end of the pier have been known to make a splash as well. Every year Seaview Pier is among the leaders in kings taken in the state, with some reaching into the forty-pound range. Other large fish include bluefish, red and black drum, cobia and tarpon.

One memorable tarpon was caught by Malcolm Condie of Newport, North Carolina, on September 17, 2008. The fish took off about four hundred yards, and about an hour later Condie landed the fish on the beach near the pier. For the first forty-five minutes he fought the fish, Condie had no idea what he was dealing with. Instead of speculating on the species, Condie just kept working it carefully to the pier. "When you hook a fish from the pier that does not mean you have him," he said. Condie had hooked and lost other tarpons, but none this large. The fish was eighty-nine inches long with a girth of forty-two inches and weighed 193.5 pounds—a new state record.

"The most amazing thing about the catch was seeing something in the water bigger than your water heater at home," he said. Three other people were needed to help him drag the record catch to his truck and lift it into the bed.

Condie's love for pier fishing is evident by what he told *Daily News* correspondent Suzanne Ulbrich. "This is another reason we need to keep the fishing piers we still have," he said. "I used to fish at the Sportsman's Pier in Atlantic Beach. It's gone. Piers give people that don't have a boat access to fishing—it's very important they be preserved."

Condie, who has lived in Carteret County all his life, started pier fishing like most people who walk the planks. In the early 1990s, he started bottom fishing at Sportsman's Pier, and then later he started plugging. He was always curious about king fishing, and in the late 1990s, he took it up and admits there is nothing like the strike of a king reeling off yards and yards of line to kick in the adrenaline.

Condie is not alone in his feelings. Piers not only offer affordable access to all, but they also offer easier access for the handicapped and less of a commitment for parents with kids who might become easily bored if the fish aren't biting. And, as Malcolm Condie would say, "You are just a strike away from having a great day."

Since being rebuilt in 1999, Seaview Pier's only major storm damage came in 2005, when Hurricane Ophelia took out a piece of Riseley Pier at Camp Lejeune and carried it down the beach to the Seaview, where it knocked out over one hundred feet of the pier. But owner Greg Ludlum had twenty-six pilings replaced, and Seaview Pier was restored to its former length.

Seaview Pier is one of the few piers that is open year-round, and it has a 150-space parking lot that can handle the weekend traffic during the fall spot run.

1984 TO 1996

By 1984, the building of new piers in North Carolina had come to a complete stop. In the previous twenty years, only four piers were built. High construction costs and new regulations regarding coastal building were making the investment in fishing piers a more marginalized business proposition. On top of that, there was the fact that most areas now had enough piers to satisfy what was essentially a steady number of fishermen.

While there was no new construction, the coast was not losing many piers. In 1984, only three piers were out of commission—Fisherman's Steel Pier (closed since 1977), New River Inlet Pier and Dolphin Pier. In the mid-1980s, both of the closed Topsail Island piers (New River Inlet and Dolphin) were still standing, and there was considerable discussion concerning their repair and possible reopening. Paradise Pier had not yet caught fire, so this short-lived moment was likely the high-water mark for the number of fishing piers in the state.

With Riseley Pier at Camp Lejeune being converted to a fishing pier in 1984, and the opening of Seaview (or Salty's) Pier, the state had thirty-five piers from which anglers could pursue their passion. Eight were on Bogue Banks, seven on Topsail Island and five on the northern Outer Banks. Hatteras and Oak Islands had three each as well.

Fishing was still good at this time. In response to indications of declining fish stocks in certain species, some regulations had started to creep in, and there was a discussion of a recreational saltwater fishing license. Conflicts between recreational and commercial fishermen arose, but no more than there had been before. All in all, there seemed to be more than enough fish to go around.

While there was an increase in pier visitors during the summer months, the fall months remained the peak time for pier fishing. Spot runs could still last for days or weeks. The large bluefish and red drum were declining but still around in good numbers, especially in the fall. Kings, tarpon and other larger fish were also at their peak in the autumn.

Even though the infamous Ash Wednesday Storm in 1962 was rough on the Outer Banks, no hurricane remotely approaching Hazel's wrath had hit the state in over twenty-five years. But as the 1970s came to a close, hurricanes were again becoming a concern. David, a Category 5 storm and the first hurricane name to be retired, swept up the Carolina coast in 1979. In 1984, Hurricane Diana damaged piers in the southeast section of the state, and a year later, Hurricane Gloria made landfall on the Outer Banks.

In 1989, Hurricane Hugo came ashore September 22 just north of Charleston, South Carolina, as an extremely large Category 4 storm packing a twenty-foot surge. Hugo was responsible for twenty-one deaths in the mainland United States. Damage estimates were $7 billion in the mainland United States. Hugo did major damage to the piers in the southeast part of North Carolina and then continued inland, causing flooding as far inland as Charlotte.

Hurricane Hugo left some pier owners scratching their heads regarding the sanity of operating a business over the open ocean, but remarkably, every damaged pier was eventually put back into operation—just as they had been after Hazel, the Ash Wednesday Storm and every other ocean-spawned weather event.

Chapter 5

Hurricane Alley Meets a Storm Surge in Real Estate

1996–2008

"Hurricane Alley" Returns

The storms of the 1980s were prepping the coast for the 1990s and a return to the days of more frequent, destructive tropical cyclones.

In 1991, Hurricane Bob traveled up the entire North Carolina coast. In 1992, Tropical Storm Danielle scraped the northern Outer Banks. In 1993, the Outer Banks were hit hard when Hurricane Emily made landfall within miles of Cape Hatteras. Flooding and wind damage were extensive on Hatteras Island.

The year 1994 saw Hurricane Gordon develop from a tropical storm to a hurricane, and then back to a tropical storm, while remaining just off the North Carolina coast. Hurricane Gordon eventually turned south before coming ashore over Florida and pushing north to the North Carolina/South Carolina state line.

In 1995, Tropical Storm Allison brushed the coast in early June. Then Hurricane Felix, a Category 4 storm, looked like it was poised to make a direct hit on the coast but suddenly turned back out to sea as Hurricane Emily had done a few years before. Felix was somewhat weakened but remained a hurricane for nine days while it sat off North Carolina's coast.

With all of the cyclonic activity that has hit the North Carolina coast over the years since L.C. Kure built the first fishing pier, it was the sister act of Hurricanes Bertha and Fran that would have the most lasting impact on North Carolina's fishing piers.

Yet, in the weeks before Bertha made landfall, pier owners and pier fishermen went about their business as they always had. The piers were open and catching fish. Fishing reports were finding their way into the *Wilmington Star News*:

May 17, 1996
- Spanish and blues at the Scotch Bonnet and Barnacle Bill's Pier
- Spots mullets and blues at the Center Pier
- Few runs of blues and Spanish at the Oceanic Pier

May 28, 1996
- Kings and Spanish caught at the Scotch Bonnet Pier.
- They are having good luck with blues and Spanish at the Oceanic Pier.
- Center reports Spanish and flounder

June 1, 1996
- Spots and mullets prevalent some nice flounder and cobia being caught as well at the Scotch Bonnet Pier.

June 7, 1996
- Nice catches of spot and some king mackerel are still being caught at the Ocean City Pier.

June 14, 1996
- Center Pier reports croaker.
- Spanish and sea mullet at the Oceanic

June 28, 1996
- Croaker and sea mullet running strong at Center Pier
- Heavy runs on small spots and blues at the Scotch Bonnet Pier
- Cobia and Spanish at the Oceanic Pier

The reports would come to an abrupt end on the afternoon of July 12, 1996, when Hurricane Bertha slammed into the coast between Wrightsville Beach and Topsail Island. Bertha was an early season Cape Verde hurricane and was the first major storm to hit North Carolina before August in ninety years. It had sustained winds of 105 miles per hour and gusts to over 144 when it made landfall.

Once over land, Hurricane Bertha lost strength and changed direction, moving to the northeast on a path parallel to the coast. The storm dumped over five inches of rain, caused $60 million in structural damage and $150 million in damage to agriculture in the state.

Fishing piers from Cape Fear to Atlantic Beach were damaged. But with Bertha arriving so early in the season, there was still a chance that the lucrative spot season could be saved, and many pier owners quickly proceeded to make repairs that would allow them to reopen their piers before the fall.

Hurricane Alley Meets a Storm Surge in Real Estate

But instead of fishermen, September would bring an even bigger storm.

In late August, another Cape Verde hurricane was forming, and by September 1 Hurricane Fran was moving quickly across the Atlantic on a path eerily similar to Bertha's. On September 5, the Category 3 storm made landfall at Cape Fear, very close to where Bertha had struck.

The worst of Hurricane Fran's wrath was felt on the north and east sides, bringing hurricane winds and rains as far up the coast as Cape Lookout and as far inland as Raleigh. On the beaches, Hurricane Bertha had taken out the protective dune, leaving nothing to slow down Fran's storm surge, which was measured at twelve feet on Topsail Island.

After landfall, Fran took a more northerly direction and produced over sixteen inches of rain across North Carolina, Virginia and West Virginia. Six people died in North Carolina, and 1.3 million people were left without power. Total damage in the state was estimated at $2 billion.

For many piers, the fishing season was over. Over half the piers in the state (nineteen) were in the path of these two storms and suffered considerable damage or were destroyed. For the few that did manage to remain open, spot season would not deliver the hoped-for revenues, as the bulk of the customers for the piers were farmers from the eastern part of the state who also suffered from the storms.

Nor'easters also did sizable damage to fishing piers in the state. Garry Oliver checking the damage at the Outer Banks Pier after a spring storm. *Courtesy of Garry Oliver.*

The 1997 season was a brief respite, but 1998 brought Hurricane Bonnie, which took a very similar path to Bertha and Fran. A Category 3 storm, Bonnie made landfall in Brunswick County, just south of Wilmington, North Carolina, and proceeded north. Hurricane Bonnie produced heavy rain and much flooding. It was also responsible for the deaths of several of the wild ponies on Shackleford Banks, which were picked up in a waterspout spawned by the hurricane.

As bad as 1996 had been, 1999 turned out to be even worse. Hurricane Dennis made landfall in August near Cedar Island as a tropical storm after threatening the coast for days as a hurricane.

Less than a month later, Category 2 Hurricane Floyd hit land at Cape Fear, in approximately same place that Hurricanes Bertha, Fran and Bonnie had. Luckily it weakened when it made landfall, but the massive storm moved slowly over the state, producing as much as nineteen inches of rain overnight. That torrent fell onto ground that was already well soaked, thanks to Hurricane Dennis. Hurricane Floyd killed fifty-seven people, mostly in eastern North Carolina, and the flooding exceeded the five-hundred-year level in nearly every river basin in the eastern part of the state.

A Storm Surge Hits Real Estate

Since the very beginning, pier owners had been regularly repairing and reopening after extensive storm damage. It was simply part of the business. That would not be the case in the years between 1997 and 2007. And, for many pier owners, the decision not to rebuild would have little or nothing to do with the weather and everything to do with a rising tide in real estate.

New factors were starting to figure into the equation and help determine whether the piers would be repaired or simply closed. Most notable of these factors was the escalating price of coastal land. For, while one might expect a sudden increase in hurricane activity to depress the value of oceanfront real estate, in the ten years from 1997 to 2007 the situation was just the opposite. Large beach houses, sometimes called "McMansions" because of their size and how fast they were built, suddenly became the vacationer's abode of choice, and they were a far cry from the first funky beach cottages that dotted the shoreline.

These houses usually rent by the week and have all the comforts of home— if your home is in Beverly Hills. Hot tubs, private swimming pools, home theaters, elevators, satellite television and wireless Internet are all available.

Hurricane Alley Meets a Storm Surge in Real Estate

The houses are large enough to occupy several families at the same time and still have room for more.

Land speculation began in earnest. Large parcels were bought up by both in-state and out-of-state development companies. Residential lots in once obscure places like Harkers Island began to change hands and escalate in price seemingly overnight. Real estate "flipping," Las Vegas style, had come to the coast. Large condo complexes, once confined to more urbanized places like Myrtle Beach and Virginia Beach, suddenly were springing up in Brunswick, New Hanover, Pender, Onslow, Carteret and Dare Counties.

As there was more vacation home and condo development, the number of motel rooms along the North Carolina coast actually declined—especially inexpensive rooms, the kind likely to be occupied by pier fishermen on vacation or down for the weekend.

Part of the changes at the coast were a natural reaction to North Carolina's increasing population, which by 2009 had reached over 9.3 million (putting us in tenth place overall, a position formerly occupied by New Jersey). However, in hindsight, it is easy to see that the building boom was part of a nationwide, and even global, economic bubble based on cheap credit and the re-packaging of mortgages. As we all have learned since 2008, the bursting of that bubble would not have a happy ending.

But at the time, the boom introduced new factors into the pier business equation. Not only were pier owners thinking twice about rebuilding after hurricanes, but they were also starting to think seriously about demolishing perfectly sound, moneymaking piers in order to cash in on the value of the real estate under the pier house and its surrounding parking lot. This is not to accuse pier owners of greed; they were simply using sound business sense.

There was a growing stack of elements beyond their control pushing pier owners to sell. For one, the cost of repairing or replacing piers had also increased. With the price of their land appreciating, taxes were also on the rise. New environmental and zoning regulations were being imposed on buildings and improvements, which added to the complexity of construction. Proposals for a new state saltwater recreational fishing license added another element of uncertainty, as some warned that this additional cost would keep people away from the piers. All of these factors made the return on the investment for the pier owner more difficult to realize.

The results came more swiftly than any dedicated pier fisherman could have predicted. After the twin storms of 1996, Emerald Isle Pier, Scotch Bonnet Pier, Ocean City Pier, Barnacle Bill's Pier and Center Pier closed their doors for good. Oceanic (Crystal) Pier, at only a fraction of its original length, allowed fishing for a few more seasons but was never again considered to be a serious fishing pier.

The Kitty Hawk Pier was next. It was damaged by Hurricane Isabel in 2003 and was finally reopened at only 220 feet in 2008. Jennette's had its last day of business at the same time, at least as a wooden, privately owned pier. It is scheduled to reopen as the first state-owned pier.

After damage from Bonnie and Floyd, the Iron Steamer Pier closed in 2000 and then reopened briefly, only to close for good in 2004. It was demolished and replaced by ten waterfront lots.

The Long Beach Pier was next. Its last day was New Years Eve 2005. According to the Associated Press, it was the victim in a divorce settlement. The AP reported, "The pier property will be divided into 10 lots worth as much as $1 million each. The Triple S closed at the end of 2005 and was already being demolished in March 2006. Its neighbor, the venerable Sportsman's, closed in October that same year. At the time, the owner, David Bradley, said that his patrons had numbered 33,000 anglers and over 100,000 sightseeing visitors a year. The pier was demolished anyway, and the land is still vacant.

The Frisco Pier was last open in 2008, and its fate remains far from certain.

After Hurricane Hugo, in 1989, Pete Herring of the Center Pier told the *Wilmington Morning Star*, "There's not much you can do about acts of God. You just have to go ahead and make the best of it."

Whether it was in response to an act of God or an offer on the table, the "best of it" for many pier owners meant getting out.

Chapter 6
The Future of Pier Fishing in North Carolina

The permanent closure of so many fishing piers happened with blazing speed. But at the same time, the public's awareness of the problem grew every time another pier was demolished. Newspapers, including the Norfolk *Virginian-Pilot*, Raleigh *News and Observer*, Charlotte *Observer* and Wilmington *Star*, all covered the story as individual piers closed. *Wildlife in North Carolina*, the official magazine of the North Carolina Wildlife Resources Commission, ran an extensive article entitled "Pier Pressure" in its June 2006 issue.

In an interview with writer Bill Morris for that story, Frank Tursi, Cape Lookout coast keeper for the North Carolina Coastal Federation, summed up the situation. "Piers are becoming like quaint historical oddities. The gentrification of the coast continues at a rapid pace, and with the piers we're losing cultural icons and access to the beach."

The conservation community was beginning to take notice, and state government in Raleigh would soon follow suit. In August 2006, the Waterfront Access Study Committee (WASC) was created by the North Carolina General Assembly and charged "to study the degree of loss and potential loss of the diversity of uses along the coastal shoreline of North Carolina, and how these losses impact access to the coastal public trust waters of the State." Urged on by public opinion and petitions circulated by fishermen and conservationists, the WASC took seriously the idea that fishing piers have long provided public access to the ocean and the beach and that the access was being threatened.

After seven months of meetings, discussions, public comments, study of waterfront-dependent uses and review of public access issues regarding coastal public trust waters, the committee determined that the state "is experiencing a significant loss in the diversity of waterfront-dependent uses and in public access."

Specific to piers, the committee came up with the following recommendations:

- That the private fishing piers providing public access be given present use value taxation classification as working waterfront. This would allow the piers to be taxed at a lower rate than if the land was valued as lots for oceanfront housing.
- That the state explore, with all due speed, sources of funding and financing mechanisms to be used to assist owners of private fishing piers with storm damage repair.
- That the North Carolina Aquariums be authorized and funded to pilot the design, development and operation of three public fishing piers.

The third recommendation built on a movement toward state-owned piers that had already begun in 2002 when the North Carolina Aquarium Society came to the rescue of Jennette's Pier in Nags Head. The Aquarium Society is a nonprofit organization that supports the North Carolina Aquariums—much as the North Carolina Symphony Society raises money in support of the North Carolina Symphony.

In 2002, the Aquarium Society had received grant money to buy and fix Jennette's—but not nearly enough money to rebuild it after Hurricane Isabel. However, by 2007, the WASC was in a position to come to the rescue with additional grant money. Funds of at least $1.7 million were made available, but first the property had to be transferred into public hands. That was accomplished by signing it over to the North Carolina Aquariums, part of the North Carolina Department of Cultural Resources.

Since that time, the "North Carolina Aquarium's Jennette's Pier" (as it will be known) has been under planning, permitting and construction. When finished, it will span one thousand feet and be made of wood set on steel-reinforced concrete pilings able to withstand hurricane winds of up to 130 miles per hour. The pier house will be sixteen thousand square feet and powered by wind and solar power.

Although there have been delays, the new pier, with its additional educational facilities, is supposed to be open to the public in May of 2011.

Emerald Isle mayor Art Schools sat on the WASC, and he has been trying to create a similar publicly owned fishing pier in his town, preferably one built on the site occupied by the Emerald Isle Pier until 1996. Since there is a state aquarium in neighboring Pine Knoll Shores, it made good sense. Planning for the pier at Emerald Isle is moving forward after the North Carolina Division of Marine Fisheries awarded the project $2.2 million from the Waterfront Access and Marine Industry (WAMI) Fund in 2008.

A similar plan is in place to have North Carolina Aquariums take over the property of the Carolina Beach Fishing Pier and connect it with the aquarium at nearby Fort Fisher. As of October 2010, the director at the North Carolina Aquarium at Fort Fisher has been working with the town manager and mayor, and a Memorandum of Agreement had been drafted. Like Jennette's, both of these new piers would be concrete rather than wood.

In 2007, Mayor Art Schools made the following prediction: "It's become my opinion that in five to ten years there will be no private piers. They're all going to be publicly owned if they're there at all. The economics just don't add up for a guy to run a fishing pier anymore without a large subsidy."

Mayor Schools's pronouncement came at the height of a coastal real estate boom. However, after the crash of 2008, demand for—and the value of—waterfront property up and down has faded. With the possible exception of the Frisco Pier (which sits on federal property anyway), no piers have closed since 2006.

This may well be just a temporary lull, and publicly funded piers may indeed be the last resort. But at a time when the state is looking at multibillion-dollar annual budget shortfalls for the foreseeable future, expect further investment in publicly funded concrete piers to come under a great deal of scrutiny, if not a sudden halt. Expect to see more headlines like this one, from the website of Raleigh TV station WRAL: "Critics say pier a symbol of misplaced priorities in a tough economy."

Despite one state-owned pier and tentative plans for two more, as the decade ends those of us who love fishing piers remain dependent on what we've always had: a few hearty souls with a passion for pier ownership, no matter what the hardships.

But regardless of their enthusiasm, we can expect that fewer piers will be rebuilt after the next big storm. The cost of rebuilding a pier has risen to a point where the return on investment could take years and is not assured. Current construction costs for piers are about $1,200 per linear foot for wood. If the pier owner would decide to build a more resilient pier and go with concrete, the cost would be $10,000 a foot. That makes a one-thousand-foot wooden pier a $1,200,000 investment.

This also means that if the end of the pier is damaged, the pier will most likely be capped and not rebuilt out to its former length. Obviously, the end result will be shorter piers.

Looking ahead to what might happen when the market for vacation homes does rebound, pier owners know that their properties fall into one of two categories.

First, there are piers that sit on ground that can be used for oceanfront housing. These piers are ripe to be sold once the economy turns. Of course, not every pier that could be developed will be. Some owners like what they are doing and have no intention of cashing out. Fortunately for the culture of North Carolina's fishermen, many owners do feel that way. But when the land finally changes hands, or the pier is damaged by a storm, the pier finds itself on shaky ground and is likely to be converted to other uses.

The second category is those that are on land that cannot be developed. These piers will not be sold for housing, as they sit on land that has likely been eroded to the point that the land will be condemned. These piers are allowed to stay and even be rebuilt because of a special building permit that forbids the land to be used for housing.

Now, after a storm, the question becomes whether the pier owner should rebuild. This question applies to both categories of piers. The answer lies in whether the owner can show a reasonable rate of return on his investment. After all, that is what he is in business for. He may love owning a pier and the people he interacts with (most owners do), and even feel he is providing a valuable service to his community (which he is) by helping to generate traffic for other businesses, but he will not be able to survive for long if he does not turn a profit.

A quick and dirty business model shows that a 750-foot wooden pier would cost about $900,000 to build. Ten dollars for a daily pass seems about average for most piers. North Carolina piers put between fifteen thousand and twenty-five thousand anglers over the water during the fishing season. Using these numbers, a pier can expect to generate revenues in the neighborhood of $150,000 to $250,000. If you ignore the others costs and revenue streams for a moment, that makes the payback on the investment somewhere in the three-and-a-half- to six-year range.

Not that bad, unless you consider the environment over which you are putting your "moneymaker." Mike Stanley told Bill Morris in his story in the *Wildlife in North Carolina*, "Putting a million dollars worth of lumber into the ocean may not be the smartest thing to do. We're the biggest gamblers this side of Las Vegas."

The Future of Pier Fishing in North Carolina

Stanley is right. Not only is it a gamble, but few, if any, piers are insured for what they have over the water. The pier house and its contents are insured, but the premium and the deductible make having insurance unattainable for the pier's boards, which are the hardest to replace and the ones that attract the angler.

Of course, savvy pier owners know that the pier gives them a chance at other revenues that would not be possible if they didn't have a pier. Bait, tackle, gear rental, snacks and drinks are all needed by fishermen. Well-stocked gift shops and T-shirt shops are moneymakers, too. Restaurants or grills also do very well. For the most part, when people show up at the pier, they are committed for a block of time and, if the fish are biting, will be reluctant to leave. Having what they need and want and being fairly priced can go a long way with paying back the investment.

Having everything you need for your patrons, including a scale to weigh that remarkable catch, is essential for the success of any pier business. Inside the pier house at Johnnie Mercer's Pier from the early 1960s. *Courtesy of Matt Johnson.*

It would be very elementary to just focus on the revenue side. There are other costs that make up the initial investment. A pier is built for $900,000, but you still have to add a pier house and buy insurance on it and the inventory. The owner has to pay his real estate taxes and get his fishing licenses. Operating expenses would include utilities, labor and repairs.

Bad weather, poor fishing and bad publicity can affect the crowds at the pier. Sometimes all three of these factors are out of the pier operator's hands. In the age of message boards and electronic mail, one bad experience can suddenly translate to a posting that is read by thousands of fishermen.

There is definitely more to it than selling worms and stapling a pass to the next fisherman's hat.

Bibliography

Most of the information contained in this book comes from the author's experiences, observations and conversations concerning subjects detailed in the book. Some other information and stories were obtained by e-mails and letters sent by NCFPS members of their experiences. Reference materials consulted include the following works by these very talented writers:

Associated Press Reports. "Bostic Battles Coastal Regulators." *Wilmington Morning Star*, March 8, 1987: 3C.

Barnes, Jay. "Lured In." *Our State Magazine* July 2007, 37–42.

———. *North Carolina Hurricane History*. Chapel Hill: University of North Carolina Press, 2001.

Bunyea, Charley. "Phoenix-Like Jennette's Pier Once Again Reborn." *Outer Banks Sentinel*, March 23, 2006: 1A.

Cantwell, Si. "Preserving Piers." *Wilmington Star-News*, May 28, 2007: 1D.

———. "Return of Pier Brings Back Memories Too Good to Lose." *Wrightsville Beach Merchant's Web of Commerce*. N.p., June 2, 2002.

Charlotte Observer. "High Cotton Snatches Lead in Governor's Cup Series." May 27, 1999: 8B.

———. "Top Catches Reeling in New Records." October 1, 1991: 17D.

Christner, Henry. "Clarkson Catch Surpasses Record." *Richmond Times Dispatch*, July 1, 1994: D-4.

———. "If Swearing Fails, Try Attitude Change." *Richmond Times Dispatch*, July 12, 1992: D-11.

Cline, Ned. *The Walter Davis Story.* Chapel Hill, NC: privately printed by Jo Ann Davis, 2009.

Cooney, Gerald. "Angler Catches Third Tarpon at Topsail." *Wilmington Morning Star*, August 12, 1983: 3D.

———. "Angler Must Adjust Times." *Wilmington Morning Star*, June 26, 1985: 4D.

———. "Anglers May Find June Pleasing Due to Diversity of Fish Available." *Wilmington Morning Star*, June 5, 1981: 3D.

———. "Big Sailfish, King Caught." *Wilmington Morning Star*, August 24, 1984: 3D.

———. "Fisher Recall's Floundering Around on Mercer's Pier." *Wilmington Morning Star*, January 8, 1989: 7B.

———. "Inshore Fishing Beginning to Slow." *Wilmington Morning Star*, June 26, 1981: 4D.

———. "Possible Record Flounder Caught in New Hanover." *Wilmington Morning Star*, November 6, 1980: 3D.

———. "Powell Lands 19-Pound Bluefish at Scotch Bonnet." *Wilmington Morning Star*, November 13, 1980: 4D.

———. "Spanish Mackerel Are Showing Up Inshore, Offshore." *Wilmington Morning Star*, June 19, 1980: 4D.

———. "Spanish Mackerel Arrive on North Carolina Coast." *Wilmington Morning Star*, June 14, 1985: 4D.

———. "Summer Doldrums Haven't Struck Coastal Fishing." *Wilmington Morning Star*, July 10, 1980: 4D.

———. "Tarpon Caught Off Crystal Pier." *Wilmington Morning Star*, July 17, 1983: 8D.

———. "Weather Cooperates for Marlin Tourney." *Wilmington Morning Star*, June 4, 1982: 3D.

DeBlieu, Jan. *Hatteras Journal.* Golden, CO: Fulcrum Incorporated, 1987.

Dilsaver, Jerry. "From Tripletail to Mullet Frenzy to Dove Hunting." *CarolinaCoast Online*, September 11, 2009.

———. "Pending State Record Tarpon Landed at Topsail Island Pier." *North Carolina Sportsman*, September 2008.

Downing, Sarah. *101 Glimpses of Nags Head.* Charleston, SC: The History Press, 2009.

———. *Vintage Outer Banks: Shifting Sands & Bygone Beaches.* Charleston, SC: The History Press, 2009.

Foster, Ken. "Area Angler Becomes 'King' for a Day." *Wilmington Morning Star*, May 8, 1998: 6C.

Goldstein, Robert J. *Coastal Fishing in the Carolinas: From Surf, Pier and Jetty.* Winston-Salem, NC: John F. Blair, Publisher, 1986.

———. *Pier Fishing in North Carolina.* Winston-Salem, NC: John F. Blair, Publisher, 1978.

Hervey, Phillip. "Body Found in Ocean." *Wilmington Morning Star*, May 10, 1994: 1B.

Holden, John F. *Holden Beach History.* Wilmington, NC: New Hanover Printing and Publishing Company, 1988.

Hooks, Jerry. "Odd Happenings at Kure Pier." *Wilmington Morning Star*, June 26, 1985: 1D.

Howard, William. "Officer Praised for Saving Girl from Surf." *Wilmington Morning Star*, August 7, 1985: 2C.

Judd, Terry. "Turnabout!" *Wilmington Morning Star*, July 8, 1978: 1B.

King, Benny. *Fishing Piers in America.* St. Peters, MO: 401 Press, 2008.

Lawson, John. *A New Journey to Carolina.* London: Echo Library, 1709.

McAllister, Ray. *Hatteras Island: Keeper of the Outer Banks.* Winston-Salem, NC: John F. Blair, Publisher, 2009.

———. *Topsail Island: Mayberry by the Sea.* Winston-Salem, NC: John F. Blair, Publisher, 2006.

———. *Wrightsville Beach: The Luminous Island.* Winston-Salem, NC: John F. Blair, Publisher, 2007.

McDonald, Bill. "Pier Anglers, Charter Boats Reports Good Fishing." *Wilmington Morning Star*, July 7, 1972: 1D.

———. "The Sea Is Generous in Yielding Fall Harvest." *Wilmington Morning Star*, October 1, 1978: 9C.

McGuire, Kim. "Immigrant Found Recipe for Success." *Wilmington Morning Star*, July 24, 1983: 1B.

Morris, Bill. "Angelo DePaola—The Fishing Marine." *The Spectator*, August 1994: 4–8.

———. "A Jury of Piers." *The Spectator*, September 1990: 14–19.

———. "Pier Pressure." *Wildlife in North Carolina*, June 2006: 22–27.

———. "Piers Lose More Ground." *Raleigh News and Observer*, April 6, 2006: 7C.

———. "Stumping for the Planks." *Raleigh News and Observer*, October 25, 2007: 7C–8C.

Nolan, Irene. "Frisco Pier Unlikely to Open This Season." *Island Free Press*, May 28, 2010.

Outlaw, Edward R., Jr. *Old Nags Head.* Norfolk, VA: Liskey Lithograph Corp., 1952.

Pippin, Jannette. "Triple S Demolition Sends Pier to Coastal Graveyard." *redOrbit*, March 9, 2006.

Rubin, Richard. "Sightseers Soared, But Pier Didn't." *Wilmington Morning Star*, November 17, 1986: 1C.

Schaver, Mark. "Pier Owners Still Rebounding After Hugo." *Wilmington Morning Star*, April 21, 1990: 2C.

Scott, Sam. "Tide Running Out for Beach Motels." *Wilmington Star-News*, March 29, 2007: 1D–2D.

Smith, Rob. "S.S. Pevensey: A Stealth Machine of the Confederacy." *A Preliminary Archaeological Assessment of the "Iron Steamer" Wreck, Sunk at Pine Knoll Shores, NC.* Special Report. January 26, 2003.

Stallman, David A. *Echoes of Topsail.* Sugarcreek, OH: Echoes Press, 2004.

Stick, David. *The Ash Wednesday Storm.* Kill Devil Hills, NC: Gresham Publications, 1987.

———. *The Outer Banks of North Carolina 1584–1958.* Chapel Hill: University of North Carolina Press, 1958.

Vance, Merton. "Motel Expansion Could Kill Condo Plans." *Wilmington Morning Star*, November 5, 1985: 1C.

Weigl, Andrea. "Ocean City a Unique Part of N.C. Coast." *Charlotte Observer*, September 8, 2009: 3B.

Wilmington Morning Star. "Area Piers Take Beating But Fishing Won't Wait." October 9, 1989: 1.

———. "Fishing Boat Rams Crystal Pier." August 9, 1980: 2A.

———. "Retired Colonel Hooks Large Tarpon." July 21, 1973: 5C.

———. "10-Year-Old Robbie Morgan Lands 40-Pound Amberjack at Topsail." July 31, 1981.

Wilson, Jim. "Coastal Tension." *Wildlife in North Carolina*, November 2006: 4–10.

Wilson, Mary. "Prosecutors: Whitten Fled the Country." *Wilmington Morning Star*, September 11, 1986: 1C.

Winegar, Garvey. "Bluefish Blitz Kitty Hawk." *Richmond Times-Dispatch*, November 20, 1987: C5.

———. "Supply of Blues Along East Coast Won't Last Forever." *Richmond Times-Dispatch*, November 28, 1989: C4.

Wirszyla, Carole. "Wrightsville Beach Piers." *Wrightsville Beach Magazine*, May 2008.

www.avalonpier.com.

www.bogueinletpier.com.

www.kurebeachfishingpier.com.

www.oceancrestpier.net.

Wyche, Ray. "The Vesta Is Buried." *Star-News*, January 7, 1973: 12-A.

About the Author

Al Baird resides in Fort Mill, South Carolina, with his wife, Mary, and their two children, Katie and Chris. He began fishing the North Carolina coast as a child in the 1960s when his family would go on their annual family vacation there. Jennette's Pier was the first pier he ever fished. In 2005, he started the North Carolina Fishing Pier Society to promote pier fishing in the state. In 2006 and 2007, he conducted a weeklong fishing pier marathon, during which he fished every pier in the state.

In 2008, he co-founded, with Mike Marsh, the North Carolina Public Access Foundation, a nonprofit organization that is dedicated to preserving access to North Carolina's natural resources.

Visit us at

www.historypress.net